The Foundation Book of Primes

By

F. Dot

ISBN: 1-4107-7439-2 (e-book)
ISBN: 1-4107-7438-4 (Paperback)

This book is printed on acid free paper.

1stBooks - rev. 09/25/03

Dedication

This book is dedicated to my family and friends who helped me during a period of almost complete destitution. Without their help, no book that I authored would every have been published. The elite tried to condemn me and extinguish my livelihood for not subscribing to their beliefs based on privileges and lordships of the few. For these elite who found it preferable to condemn and exclude, the same fate awaits you! However, I will be disappointing them. My focus will be on the birth and growth of a sentient movement that will bring environments for those who seek to develop their abilities towards universal awareness and atonement. I am deeply grateful to wise thinking sentient predecessors whom, unbeknownst to them, have helped me with this book's prime foundation.

Table of Contents

Chapters

Introduction

First Edition

This first edition was composed and released without delay so that the pentarchy prime founders can have a starter set in which to accelerate the premiere foundation prime construction. This author didn't want to get in the way of sentients making initial contact with one another anxious to get started by delaying the book's release any longer than necessary. A spectacular world awaits all of you. It is okay to be dazzled. Take care and enjoy your journey.

An Her-Storical Reference

This book in time, will be a her-storical (historical) one. It will be a snapshot as to how far we have all come from a particular point in time. For us here and now, the reference is why are we taking so long? Be patient. Changes are frightening to most inhabitants. The war they fight will be their own and not of ours.

I am a product of—

A nation-state may make a claim that the author is a product of their favorable environment. The truth of the matter is that there were those who tried to destroy or greatly limit the author's existence and pursuits due to her view of not adhering to prevailing dogma. To have only a corporeal view will keep one in the material realm. There is much more than meets the eye. Take a chance and "see" for yourself.

Super Power Status is fleeting

The contents of this book may be viewed as unnecessary due to the fact that a super power nation-state exists today. Actually, its existence is fleeting because of its forced exclusionary laws that chip away at its power. These same laws are their downfall. History provides numerous examples of this. Are you prime for a universal framework?

Written Now

This book is being written now so that when major Earth changes occur, this handbook will allow order to quickly be established. Relying on arcane institutions will extend harsh pain and suffering. This is unnecessary. We have the capability to provide caring and humane treatment towards each other. Do not be fooled when others make the claim that the current belief systems are the only ones. Dare to choose a more all encompassing one.

Blue Print for Development

This book is provided as a blue print for an optimum environment for advancing entity pools' development. One of the purposes is to describe a framework for all sentients to be included, if the will be there. The framework is one of inclusion and not to be limited to a small percent of the society pool. Are you up to it?

Birth of a Framework

"An initial birth framework" is covered in this book. Allow twenty-five continuous years with the launch of this framework before making major refinements so that the framework can take hold. True, the objective is to continuously develop (evolve) towards a state of a higher level of awareness. However, this will take time. Please be patient. Consider that a greatly refined framework may mean that it is not for an "Earth-based framework" but for another realm. Wouldn't that be marvelous?

Need a Disclaimer?

We can customize a disclaimer for you if you like should you find the words that are used in this book disturbing. The journey is truly yours to take should you choose to take a chance on something that will be quite magnificent! Do you need a disclaimer or will you dare to choose?

Historical Societal Pool View

Temporary Land Rights

Land rights only last until the next invading armed forces or when civil wars occur. This only happens when property is valued more than sentient entities. We can choose not to make this so.

Barbarism to Civilization

All countries go through barbarism before becoming "civilized", or so the view is. Their belief systems require acceptance of property rights. Acceptance yields to slavery. This is quite an ancient concept and is nothing more than government supported caste system.

Feudal Fires

Nation-states are founded by violence. Nation-states are perpetuated when there are violent oppositions. However, nations cannot exist without feudal lords. With feudal lords, all members are subjects (properties) of them. This is how a feudal system works. Consider not fueling the fires of these feudal lords.

"Smugness exhibited by feudal lords."

Subjects of the State

Every state, no matter if a union of states, owns its subjects. This is not how a great society ought to work to safeguard all members of it.

Which Came First, Law or Crime?

The historical belief is nothing more than the assumption that in order for "wise" actions to be taken, laws must first be passed. When one looks at this premise, wise actions are not taken. Feudal based laws (land lord laws) prevails. Hence, properties are owned by the state. Once laws are passed, the acts that they describe become illegal and hence, become crimes. Prior to that, these same acts are not crimes. Hence, laws are artificial concepts and not necessarily wise outcomes. Pain and suffering must be endured to be a "just" reaction!

Family Civil Wars

In recent belief systems, if a member of society is condemn, then the community—family, extend family and friends, neighbors, etc.—is condemned by this condemning action. Even without considering the unintended members, these recent belief systems support terrorism. Is this just? Elimination of terrorism begins at home. The need to get out of the terrorism business in all its forms is ever present.

Historical Societal Governance View

State Dominant Stature

The "state" is viewed as one even though there are legions of soldiers to defend this view of one. A single individual is brought before this state's view of one to stand before an army that hold the guns to her annihilation.

The Rule of Law

The rule of law requires the existence of property rights. How else can rulings be made. It is this notion that "divide and conquer" take on a purist meaning. Court cases are done when two subjects contest an agreement. Having one person sue another is not as unbalanced as having one state sue or prosecute one person. The deck is stacked against the one person, the one individual. This allows the state to do things with impunity! If it makes a mistake, no recourse for this criminal act by the state is available. One person does not have a fair playing field against the ruthless singular state.

The Law of One

In feudal laws, one is considered separate before the law. Collectives such as governments and corporations are considered separate before the law. The difference is that one entity is composed of one member of society while governments and corporations have armies to challenge and defend their way of life or existence. Indeed, these collectives defined as "single entities" hide behind the aprons of the "Law of One".

Property Rights

The nation-state belief system is based on ownership of property. The greater the real estate, the higher is the position in society. Those who are not owners of land property are then owned by their feudal lords or land lords.

By treating "citizens" as subjects of the state, then the state can go anywhere to retrieve its subjects. After all, subjects are property.

Law of the Land

Our laws only apply to citizens surrounded by nation-state boundaries when they ought to apply to all sentient beings no matter what location they are living in at any particular time. The purpose for placing borders is to define property. They are not protective barriers because these same borders have the duality of keeping subjects in, as if we are like plants and can't escape from the land that is under our feet! It should now be clear to you what the phrase "law of the land" really means.

Go Straight to Jail: Criminal/Civil Jury Awards

Jail was barbarous for less serious offenses. Sentencing was NOT universally consistent in all cases. Instead of the impact of the offense, a jail and/or probation time and/or cost penalty were applied. In this way, the rich were shielded from hardship. There was the acceptance in the notion that life is not fair. Is this your belief, too?

Prison Environment

Our prison population has gotten very large because of the increased number of laws and an "efficient" legal industry. The question ought to be asked; Are folks becoming more criminal or is our system in shambles of imploding? The latter is the case. The system breaks up communities and examines only individuals, legally classified as such, against a sea of a legal army of troops. Bullying is the order of the day, which does not provide for the common good or a caring environment.

Behavior Modification

The law is being used in behavior modification for all members of society. By using terrorism, i.e. condemnation of its subjects, then most will be sufficiently fearful to adhere to feudal lords and their artificial laws. Normally, the sentencing results in condemnation existing for an entity's entire life span.

Prison Term Waiting Period

Currently, there is at least a 30-day waiting period before arriving at a prison sentence for non-violent crimes, such is these more obedient chattel-shaping activities. If this is the case, why not place them in containment camps with minimum security? However, the current prevailing belief is to condemn. This feeds on itself. The end result is that the belief system itself is condemned.

The Right to Property

It is because of the notion of "property rights" that war is inevitable. Those without property have very little say in a nation-state (land based) boundary concept. By stripping current inhabitants of their property rights, "new lands" are discovered and "new claims of ownership" ensue. Hence, new wealth are "discovered". In actuality, prior inhabitants and caretakers have been raped and slaughtered to make room for new "free citizens".

Forced Repatriation

Terrorism is done by forced repatriation of subjects who do not want to return even when no non-entry crimes have been committed. Imagine yourself in this position!

Most Developed Nation and its Condemnation View

The "most developed nation" in the world came to recognize that their mass production of issuing sentences of condemnation was having a negative impact to their existence. More "fashionable" condemnation laws had to be passed to make it illegal to flee or resist arrest. In this way, shaping was enforced so that the entities that are condemned will not revolt and remain domesticated and docile. This most developed nation wanted all it's subjects to be in this behavioral state so as to round them up with little resistance. Executions can then be made at the final destination when it is convenient for this nation. Are you next?

Iron Curtains for Borders

The iron curtain still exists. It's called national (country) boundaries where free entities who cross are tagged as "illegals" and hence, non-citizens. They are then placed behind "iron curtains".

Carrot and Stick

Those who are privileged to information will want to retain that privilege by accepting the decisions of others that are the senior distributors of it. Hence, the shaping of the willing whom readily accepts this notion.

Labor of Profits

Those who are elitist are comfortable because they do profit off the mass labors of others. The masses are to be damned.

Patriot Games

The elite enjoy playing patriot games in their coliseum, this coliseum built by land (war) lords.

State Sanctioned Terrorism Results

Entities are condemned for life, due to a felony conviction no matter how minor the infraction or the harmful degree of the act. The view is that the state's engine of convictions and condemnations must continue no matter if it is a just system or not. No one dares stops the assembly line. Hence, the effect is that terrorism exists. The view by the state is that a tool is constructed to permit and keep feudal lords in power, licensed to condemn and sanctioned by the state.

Legal Terrorism

The recent nation-states enforce legal terrorism by excluding entities from jobs, money, access to

F. Dot

credit, and other basic needs based on serious or felony convictions no matter what that degree is or being given a "non-citizen" status even in the case when no other "crime" has been given.

Historical Justice ("Just Ice") System

Feeders to the Justice System

In recent historical "Western" systems, the legislative process feeds the judiciary process with constraints that further restrict entity pursuits. Legislative Acts are passed into law. The Executive is chartered to carry out these laws based on its interpretation of them or the vagrant disregard for the spirit of these laws. When disputes arise, then it is up to the Judiciary to arrive at final determinations. The whole process stops at the Judiciary. It does not feed any other process! However, had these artificial (man-made) laws not have violated sacred principles, the Judiciary would not be responding in a feudal way. Members of the Judiciary do have biases and are nothing more than surrogates to perpetuate the belief that the few (elite) knows what is best for the masses. In this book, the term "judiciary" or variations there of will be used to mean all of the above.

Adversarial by Nature

An adversarial system of justice that condemns innocent entities in the name of justice is flawed. To say that it is the best system that there can be is not acceptable. A replacement system can be found when the desire for something better is present. A system that does not condemn will ensure that every entity has a chance for the truth to surface in time. After all, is it not paramount that the discovery of the truth be supreme?

F. Dot

The Passing of Responsibilities

The current justice system requires that institutions exist since legislative/parliament officials are not ultimately responsible for law enforcement decisions. The preservation of institutions is paramount in this framework.

Judicial Administrators

Judges are administrators. What we need are caretakers!

The Weighing-in on Sentences

It is strange that murder or killing of another entity in human form is treated just like any other crime with sentences. They can have lighter sentences than other crimes that do not kill or gravely injure others. Releasing of those who will commit violent crimes again is a way to ensure that a chorus for law and order and the permission to expand the incarceration of others by passing additional laws is sanctioned. It is only in this way that power is retained by a few feudal lords. These same feudal lords are not capable of leading and being caretakers. They know only how to condemn. This belief system exists because of misguided believers who permit it to be so. Expect and demand something much greater to take its place!

Court Soldiers

Lawyers are officers (soldiers) of the court they serve. They are commissioned by the courts and can be de-commissioned (disbarred) when adherence to the belief system wanders. Lawyers, based on the requirements for the job, do not serve the public for fear of being terrorized (threaten to be disbarred). They are very often condemned for life once disbarred.

Lack of Prevention

The Criminal Justice System fails more times than is acknowledged. It is not an equalizer (fair) system. Bias is on the side of the privilege few, those with significant properties (assets) and elite contacts. The criminal justice system's premise is to deter (having a deterrent factor) by condemning. Prevention is not part of the system's framework. Knee-jerk reactions to events are the basis for their charter.

Sterile Automatons

Sterile-automatons are the ones that normally advance in historical systems. Are you one?

Disposal Laws

Laws are barbaric when disposal specifications to feudal subjects are defined. Civilization is not present in this framework.

Government Service

Government is a service. For matters involving major issues, this ought not to be left to few members of society to correct injustice. The resources of the few, whose passions are admirable, are limited compare to the built-in overwhelming and unlimited government ceiling design. Government ought to ensure the vibrant health of society. Having prime involvement ensures that no injustice falls through the cracks.

"Silent Discrimination" (or Closet Discrimination)

The current concept of a member of society classified as a "felon" is cruel and unusual punishment because of the edict or perspective (belief) that instead of withholding a particular set of privileges in the set of all privileges pertaining to the "crime", the edict is for all privileges. This is done by the unspoken and hidden actions of a select elite who will make this so. However, all denials can be seen and heard when the senses are keen to them. Do not be fooled.

Felons Locked Out

The current prevailing belief system of man-made laws requires that subjects of the state be in fear of exclusions. Examples, those subjects condemned with a felony are locked out of choice positions. Hence, they are restricted to a caste of low subsistence. Should there be a high degree of certainty that the offender will commit harm again, then confinement ought to be required in all cases.

Environmental Dangers Abyss

The legal system is inadequate to members subject to environmental dangers and contamination. Once exposed, the legal system premise is that members are to be responsible for taking actions to petition the courts for a court order. This is a false view. The legal system is only in place to render decisions involving business and their transactions.

Court-Based Deception

The current system of criminal justice is based on deception by the players and not based on the truth. It is overrated. It is a system of posturing. Seeking the truth is not its primary motivation; legal maneuvering is.

Bias Illusion

There is an illusion that the current justice system is fair and impartial. Nothing can be further from the truth. The warriors are made up of bias individuals whereby judicial outcomes are not uniform. The outcomes can be overturned and/or reversed. These historical references illustrate that no legal outcome is cast in stone.

"Legal Maneuvering"

Currently, laws are arbitrary. When laws have to be interpreted, the lawmakers cannot be relied on to make laws. What we have here is "legal maneuvering". This ought not to be the case.

Easy Lockup Prey of the Homeless

A very valid question is whose judicial system is it anyway? The answer may surprise you. Our current judicial system has an easier time locking up homeless "individuals" than wealthy ones. The answer is clear.

Close Enough?

As of the writing of this book, the Postal Service has a very high, close to one hundred percent, success rate for the delivery of all pieces of mail to the addressees given. The judicial system falls far shorter than one hundred percent in their success rate. We are very upset when mail is not delivered as promised than when the judicial system fails to "balance the truth" with a high degree of accuracy. The law is not blind at all, but limited by the corporeal trappings of men and women. Know this when passing judgment.

Blind Obedience

Obedience for the historical judicial system is an ongoing requirement. The truth of the matter is that not only is "lady justice" blind, but staunch believers are too!

Take Back Your Right

The judicial system exists because you gave away your right to decide. Choose to take it back. Allow the business judicial system to continue to exist in resolving business disputes in the interim. This part of the current legislative/judiciary system has been fine-tuned because of the framework premise of property and contractual rights.

An Epiphany for Sentient Pool Framework

Caught in the Web of Insights

Insights may be random events. The first impression is one that must be caught in a web of insights. However, the collection set triggers an epiphany. How wonderful this is!

Legal Protection

Even in a democratic unit or system, the law applies only to members of that unit or system. Anyone outside of it is not protected since one would be a non-member. This is exactly the policy or policies that condemn others around the world to be abused, tortured, or even put to death because of the forced policy of repatriation. Members are owned by the landowners of the feudal systems who are "rooted" in them. It is for this reason that associations ought to be governed not by land boundaries or borders but rather by the pool in which they choose to associate. The overlapping of pools will dictate the larger pool umbrella that encompasses both associations governs matters relating to this overlap.

The Reciprocal not Observe

The smug and arrogance of the Justice System is not a "just" system when it violates other systems. Tyranny rules when a belief system is forcibly imposed on another. There is insistence by a "great power" in objecting to others who violate one's air/land space. However, the reciprocal is not observed. The imperial way tramples all others.

For Insiders Only

For insiders only, a "just" system is directly
related to a particular domain. However, this
particular "just system" is null and void when it
tramples on another insiders' domain in its refusal
to recognize their form of just and equitable
systems.

In a secure corner of the world, a country that
restricts immigration does export slavery, human
bondage, and forced repatriation. These are
forerunners to executions. What is set in motion
continues in motion. The answer is to not set into
motion these terrorist acts.

Justice Monopoly

The "justice" arena is the sole monopoly of the
state. Since it is a monopoly, it ought to give
equal resources to both sides in justice cases.
However, only prosecutors have access to all of the
state's resources. A single individual is limited
by access to her personal resources, which pales to
that of the state. In this way, an individual is
singled out. A state is also considered a single
entity. Indeed it is! It is one army or legion of
judicial solders. What single individual can match
this unless a member of the elite with matching
funds?

The Few Elite

The elite will separate those who are selected from
those who are not by employing those who are and
having them at remote or secured locations, away
from the common class. Also, where the elite and
their families live are isolated because of wealth.
In this way, the selected ones will only know and
experience good things and not be troubled by lower

class problems. For them, understanding the plight of others who are not selected and are struggling is very difficult for them. Since there are instances of rages to riches, the belief is that anyone can overcome obstacles. These are relatively rare and the selection is for the most gifted. The vast majority will continue their struggles most of their lives.

The Inclusion View of Being a Citizen

In western law of "great nation-states", only "citizens" of the feudal state can have rights. The definition is specific. If certain groups or pools are not included, then no rights exist for them. In that narrow interpretation, anything can and is done to non-citizens. For example, children are property of custodians, which very often are awarded to women. Unborn children are always property of the mothers with no state-defined person-hood status to be disposed of at will and are in fact made. They are non-citizens. How convenient it is for a state to dispose of property.

History shows that other living groups were considered non-citizens. Recall what happen to the plight of the Native American and slaves. Also, conscripts have a duty to serve. For example, serving on jury duty and the Armed Services, which in the later case are considered Government Issue (GI). In certain instances of law, killing of non-citizens, those of an "enemy nation-state", are allowed with no reprisals. In fact, opposing members of armies are always forgiven because they serve the country that issued the order. If this were not the case, then the state would have to condemn its own armies for crimes that could have been imposed by opposing forces. How convenient this is. In the aftermath of wars, the opposing country must make accounting for all soldiers missing-in-action before diplomatic talks can continue by the "greatest western nation-state". Since many acts of wars have normally been done on foreign soil, our accounting of opposing army soldiers missing-in-action is of little consequence.

Terrorism

If countries profess that citizens should be free to travel at will, then why do these same countries prevent the admittance of others? They are "non-citizens", which are not given the same rights and privileges as are given to "citizens". In this manner, these "exclusive" countries are parties to atrocities. In fact, those evil counties did learn historical lessons from those self-professed democratic sovereign states by suppressing their own people and also the torturing and murdering of members of their respective sovereign states. We condemn them because they are non-citizens. This is tantamount to terrorism. Many will say that this is not so. However, they are not blameless because they will on a regular basis forbid the entry of non-citizens. The proof is always on the fleeing people to show that they are in danger. Our history shows that we commonly performed force repatriation (return) of fleeing citizens of the world only to learn later that our actions caused much suffering and death. Many who profess in being honorable people did in fact condemn others and hence, were participants to atrocities.

Reign of Terror by any other Name

Historical legislative/executive/judicial systems provided an apron for the reign of terror for its members with an adherence to their system of condemning. Once condemned, an entity is locked out of the societal pool for life, way beyond the term limits of the sentence. This framework can easily be replaced.

Plants Have No Mobility

Plants have no mobility. They are rooted in land. We are not plants. Our legs are not implanted into the ground. We are mobile. It is only natural that our systems must also include mobility as a basic tenet. The notion of the law of the land forces us to be like plants. However, to thrive means to have systems in place that are vanguards to mobility.

The True Duration of a Sentence

The concept of prison sentences dictates the duration for the punishment of a crime. The person is then free when the duration is completed. However, implementation by the law belief system is to not be free of association for an entire life!

The Export of Terror

Exporting terrorism is the result of denying passage through nation-state boundaries by non-citizens.

Barriers of Enslavement

When barriers purposely constructed to block mobility of sentient beings, the ultimate goal by those who constructed these barriers is to enslave us all. To the non-chosen few, tear down these walls!

Class System

When accommodations are primarily given to feudal governmental members to the consternation of the vast majority of members who also contribute promotes a class (caste) system. One class is of privilege while the other classes are damned. We perpetuate this view still.

Stalled Corrective Actions

Our recent system of government, legislative/executive/judicial, cannot handle mistakes in their own decisions very well. It is hard for this framework to take speedy corrective actions. This is not surprising since it is artificial (man-made). Time delays are built-in and not naturally based.

It Can Happen to You

It can happen to anyone. It doesn't matter how good your character is. Once the state tags you, labels you, condemns you, the inferior classification stays with you for life. The question that ought to be asked is this. Is the state a valid institution? The answer lies within you. How do you choose?

"Neighbor Papers" Needed

Neighbors need not require papers to pass through the neighborhood. Neighboring states ought to be no different. Travel papers is an evidentiary indication of inferiority. The implied message is this: "We don't want them in our neighborhood!"

Secure National Borders

There are those who believe in a secure nation-state border as the way to provide for security. This belief will place you on the other side of the fence looking in, which may not be that evident in the here and now. Earth events have a way of cleaning house to correct imbalances.

"Legal and Just" Captivity

One may think that laws are just. It is not when laws have the effect of executing and/or gravely harming entities in captivity. The result is that laws become very unjust. Think about it for a while before coming to your conclusion.

Condemned for Life!

We do not have a humane and just system of justice when it condemns entities for life through its decree. All other institutions and businesses follow this lead. One might say that it is "a stamp of disapproval and discard".

Feudal State Believers

The feudal state needs enough believers to sustain it. Therefore, those who feed its belly promotes its abuses and your misfortunes.

Ideal Power Concentration Objective

Concentration of power to a few, this is the ideal with feudal lords. What are your chances of becoming a member of this exclusive club?

The law kills

The law kills. If this were not so, then why are there state-sanctioned executions? Supposedly, there are laws against killings. Apparently, the states are exempt. How fair is this? As with other things, the state has a monopoly. Terrorism is the result of all monopolies.

Children as Property!

Children are the property of guardians, even when children are abused and may then become homeless. They are in limbo because the nation-state laws make it illegal to help them without guardian approval. Housing, caring, or providing them with jobs often leads those who do with nation-state prosecutions and sentencing.

Protection of Property

The historical belief system regarding governance is flawed. The premise is that members of society are properties of land-based nation-states. In practice, members are properties of land lords. Democratic belief systems are no different. These systems have exclusionary "laws" (man-made). Non-citizens are excluded. This leads to systems that promote terrorism everywhere.

The Inner Circle

The elite require members be in the inner circle for consideration of privileges. The inner circle is small compared to the entire pool. When the pool finally choose to make decisions for themselves, the inner circle framework will implode and cease to exist because the pool will no longer fund and grant authority to it. A leader caretaker-based framework will require the admittance of all that advocate non-violence. With the inner circle, it requires force to keep the greater pool at bay.

The Thinning of Military Nation-States

It has been said that a superior military machine insures a protected nation-state to exist by keeping other nation-states and their subjects confined. There is something even more superior, which doesn't require any military machine at all. Allow any sentient entity safe passage through our environments who migrated out of repressive and very harmful environments. Oppressive and abusive nation-states will be "de-selected" into oblivion with this escape tenet. The military machines will likewise follow the same fate.

The Tightening of the Albatross Laws

When new inventions and ideas are first introduced into society, no laws exist to suppress them. After a while, laws are introduced that generally are never reversed and become albatrosses on individuals. This leads to suffocation. To be alive, we breathe in and out. Our laws ought to do likewise. Loosen them up when breathing is impaired.

Systems of Exclusions

The historical belief systems of the world are based on exclusions. With this, how can they possible be just?

Slavery Preserved

To be all things to all people is the bottleneck of the current belief system. The few elite who decides on behalf of the masses ensures the preservation of land lords and their subjects. This is just another name for slavery.

Free Trade Only?

When it comes to commerce between nation-states, free trade is permissible. The same cannot be said for free passage of entities. Why is that so? Do goods and services have more "value" than sentients?

Terminal Affect

Terminating entities through exclusions. On may term this the "terminal affect".

Exclusion is Terrorism!

You need more convincing? Stick around.

The Nooses of Nation-States

The concept of nation-states will return to the ocean just like before the "dawn" of nation-states. History has recorded that great nation-states did occur at different times. Each has imploded in its own noose of tighter and tighter elite domains. In time, the weight of those who are excluded will be too great to carry. We don't have to wait for these events to happen when the will is there.

Self-Restricting Noose

The harder the elite forces a more restrictive environment, the more they place a noose around their own necks. This is always the outcome. Do not be fooled by those who say otherwise. Stick around and see for yourself.

Criminal Activity Inclusive

A criminal activity can be based on natural law. To say that criminal activities can be based only on man-made (artificial) laws is folly. In the latter, a law has to be passed before a naturally recognized law regarding harmful acts can be considered a "crime". Why wait for this to happen?

It Started with Good Intentions

You are still subscribing to a belief system enforced by a small geographical country of this world. Why are you allowing the state known as "The Greatest Nation on Earth" to dictate terms and conditions for the entire world? Many good intentional civilizations in history also dictated the terms and conditions to the known world, too. The enforcement was done through exclusion of a great majority of peoples. Today, we are again experiencing the same. Your support for this is allowing a small country in size as a relation to the entire Earth to rule the world. Take responsibility for your actions. The numbers are on your side should you choose to have yourself counted as well.

"I still believe!" Why?

So many people still believe in the historical (artifact) system and still cannot understand why there are still are (real estate) wars. Change to a different system. Adopt a border-absent system and the wars and related industries will no longer be needed to resolve land disputes.

Not that Complex

There is a belief that to govern is complex and difficult. This view promotes in-decisions and in-actions. Actually, what is needed is for wise directives of prime importance to be made. This requires wise leader caretakers to be recognized.

Multiplicity

Recent history illustrates that what we have is not "duplicity" of action and in-action, but "multiplicity" of the same. Multiplicity exists with the many overlapping governmental organizations. Is there any wonder that there is confusion and hesitation in making wise decisions and activities? A clear singular umbrella approach is the wisest.

Invitation to an Association

An invitation is truly an invitation when the one who is being invited has the option to decline. Otherwise, one is a conscript. It is wise not to recognize a belief that imprisons people for their own beliefs and free choices in the association with others as long as it does not violates another person's free association.

Time of Earth-Holdings Changes

When major Earth changes arrive in our time, there will be those who will still have property and those who lost theirs because of these changes. Will this lead to great disturbances? If you cling to the law of property, to have property and power means the servitude, slavery, and at times, torture of others who do not. Eventually, the prevailing feudal system will be replaced with a more equitable one.

Together, We Survive

Something very interesting happens with a well-oiled machine. When there is no one to oil the machine, it slows down and eventually stops all together. The damage done by not oiling it may be beyond repair. Making this so will direct us to rely on one another to ensure a natural subsistence environment.

That Which Is!

Forms of terrorism are not how states defined them, but in actuality, that which is. Consider keeping them in check wherever you find them.

Can be kept in Check

Society can stop any abusive demagogue/politician in her tracks, if the will be there. Experts may think they know what to do until society sets them right.

The Labors of Others

Throughout history, wealth, by and large, is always obtained by the labors of others. Are we caretakers of the few or the many?

Why Subscribe

Why must one subscribe to the notion that nation-states own its citizens? This promotes servitude to land lords. This promotes taxation for real estate. This promotes wars by land (war) lords.

Political Systems Rigidity

Historically, the political systems are too rigid to allow for diversity. A system based on diversity will yield the greatest solutions to contemporary issues. This can only be done through inclusion of all. Hence, political systems are doomed.

Impediments to World Peace

Nation-states are the impediments to world peace and tranquillity. Their need to hoard land and resources is their motivation. The inhabitants in all their diversities are to be damned. What kind of environment do we want to live in?

Transitional Decriminalization

Examining history, when psychology was in its infancy, increasing the number of mental institutions was viewed as the proper thing to do. Over time, it then was realized that we were locking up well-balanced persons. So we released a lot of persons back into society. In similar ways, we are locking up a high percentage of well-balanced persons. We need to decriminalize many laws that made criminals of them. Self-determination and expressions, as long as these activities and actions do not adversely affect other members, will not be described as criminal acts. The safety and well being of sentient beings are two of the paramount concerns of a true civilized society.

The Burden Lifted

We will lift the burden of the few in making decisions when they affect us all. The burden will instead be placed on the multitudes. In this way, all will benefit from our decisions.

Non-Citizen Classification

Historically, groups (races) of sentient beings can be classified as non-citizens. The view from Earth's perspective is that we are all citizens of Earth. Therefore, in no case will sentient beings be classified as non-citizens or as non-members. To decide otherwise will result in the Earth's sphere of correcting the imbalances.

Expanding Sentient Inclusion

Historically, the notion of what is human is defined as *Homo sapiens*. Anything else is viewed as non-sentient. There may have been contacts with other forms but they were expelled or eliminated because of denial of these other forms. What needs to happen is that members in a society are defined and included based on characteristics of being sentient and not by being *Homo sapiens* exclusively. Acceptance of all that exhibit sentient awareness is the first major step towards one's own higher awareness. This next step is within reach, should wisdom prevail.

F. Dot

Self-Initiated Borders

There are no national borders, only self initiated borders to your own experiences.

Preamble to Pentarchy Prime

A Higher Awareness Charter

Anew charter will be adopted that will aid sentients into a higher level of awareness while inhabitants in our environments. The charter is described in this book starting with the following preamble.

Preamble to Pentarchy Prime

It is with supreme inspiration that this sentient directing charter is drafted and accepted in order for the inhabitants of Earth and all other discovered worlds to integrate effectively, in this era of sentient awareness with one another. We understand that each sojourner is within worldly influences and at her unique level of awareness. No law is valid which states otherwise. Everyone is created equal in the realization that each one of us yearns to grow and develop in ways that will brighten the spirit-soul to the journey back from whence we came. We understand that we have lost our way and All-That-Is (ATI) has provided a way to gain back that knowledge and insight. We recognize that sentient entities have various capabilities and capacities to help and assist others in their development and that the supreme spiritual path is to be the caretakers of others. For it is by this pursuit that our journey back to ATI is assured.

An Epiphany for a Pentarchy Prime Model

To Grasp a Greater Society

We are all made in our creator's image. While in an Earth's sphere of influence as part of our spiritually expanding experiences, we are given an environment that best meets our needs at this present time. The clues for optimum vitality are ever present. Take our body, for example. We have two hands, each having four fingers and a commanding thumb. The thumb is larger and positioned quite distinctly different from the other four fingers. The hand utilizing all fingers and the thumb can grasp extremely well many different kinds of material objects. With this observation in mind, it is being stated here without rigorous discussion or validation that an advanced quantum leap to a greater foundation society can occur by implementing the following governing framework.

Prime Degrees or Power Primes

Initiate and select on an individual entity free spirited basis an association or pool comprised of a total of five members that closely identifies with the entity based on the other members of the association or pool who share the same identification. The members agree to bind in the pursuit of achieving collective harmony and purpose. This association or pool is called the Premiere Foundation Pentarchy Prime. The more detailed mechanics for association will be described elsewhere. From the five, one representative leader will be selected to speak on behalf of the foundation pentarchy prime in matters affecting their pentarchy prime. The leader will then form an association with four other leaders at the same pentarchy prime degree to form the next ascension pentarchy prime. The members agree to bind in the pursuit of achieving collective harmony and purpose, the same premise as the foundation pentarchy prime. From the five, one representative leader will be selected to speak on behalf of the ascension pentarchy prime in matters affecting their pentarchy prime. The leader will then form an association with four other leaders at the same pentarchy prime degree to form the next ascension pentarchy prime. This process repeats until the apex pentarchy prime is achieved whereby every foundation pentarchy prime is a descendent of one of the representative leader caretakers of the apex pentarchy prime. The proper name for this prime is the Sentient Nexus Pentarchy Prime. The premise for each degree of pentarchy primes is to wisely derive decisions encompassing all members under its umbrella on matters involving two or more degree minus-one foundation primes for a particular degree pentarchy prime.

Pentarchy Prime Associations

Let's start with building blocks. Start with group associations of five and allow them to be autonomous in their affairs dealing with one another in this pool. Provide complete respect for a group to exist apart from other groups.

Ebb and flow of associations, this reflects the natural order of existence.

F. Dot

Power Prime Matrices

Let's look at each pentarchy prime degrees of five member entities.

```
Prime Matrix  1: 5 to the first power     = 5
Prime Matrix  2: 5 to the second power    = 25
Prime Matrix  3: 5 to the third power     = 125
Prime Matrix  4: 5 to the forth power     = 625
Prime Matrix  5: 5 to the fifth power     = 3,125
Prime Matrix  6: 5 to the sixth power     = 15,625
Prime Matrix  7: 5 to the seventh power   = 78,125
Prime Matrix  8: 5 to the eighth power    = 390,625
Prime Matrix  9: 5 to the ninth power     = 1,953,125
Prime Matrix 10: 5 to the tenth power     = 9,765,625
Prime Matrix 11: 5 to the eleventh power  = 48,828,125
Prime Matrix 12: 5 to the twelfth power   = 244,140,625
Prime Matrix 13: 5 to the thirteenth power = 1,220,703,125
Prime Matrix 14: 5 to the fourteenth power = 6,103,515,625
Prime Matrix 15: 5 to the fifteenth power  = 30,517,578,125
```

Note: The primary digit always identifies a pentarchy prime with the numeral five. A Universe Prime Power Designation is used to represent each prime power degree.

Optimum Participation

It starts with an association of five to have optimum discussions and then generate decisions on matters of importance to the association. When matters deal with only the association, then that association is given the empowerment to shape the outcome of the item. All external associations will have no jurisdiction to overrule the association in question. From five associations, a higher association will be formed from the selection of one member by each of the five associations. This higher association will have jurisdiction over matters that overlap the interactions of two or more of the primary associations. When two up to five associations at the second degree have formed, then a third-degree association is formed from a member of each of the second-degree associations. Matters handled at these third-degree associations will be for items that affect two or more of the second-degree associations. This process is repeated until the greatest association-degree umbrella can handle matters encompassing every member that is discovered. The guideline above pertaining to two up to five association. It requires five associations should that number exist. In the beginning, there may only be two, three, or four associations that have formed and no other.

When selecting a pool leader, choose wisely.

Prime Designation

Use "degree" prime designation to describe ascension levels of primes being considered.

From Foundation to the Nexus

The first power prime is given the term "Premiere Foundation" since all other pentarchy primes are built on this solid base. Each ascension degree association must effectively represent the number of entities given in the table above. By examining the table above, the fifteenth pentarchy prime degree represents approximately 31 billion entities! The highest degree power prime will be termed the "Sentient Nexus" because it will be closest to All-That-Is!

Bequeathing Caretaking to the Next Ascension Pentarchy Prime

In the pentarchy primes of society, governing rules at the next ascension pentarchy prime can only be defined and implemented when they are delegated by

all five foundation pentarchy primes. Another way
involves the exchange of members in at least two of
the five foundation pentarchy primes of a
particular ascension prime.

Leader Caretakers' Validation

Leader caretakers are not selected by popular vote.
Validation at every pentarchy prime degree
selection is required. In this way, a leader
caretaker is intimately aware of concerns at every
degree within her umbrella.

*Take ownership of decisions. Choose your caretakers
wisely.*

Matters Affecting the Prime

The process of ascension (degree) prime formation
is repeated as long as there are still primes,
which is to say that sufficient need to go even
further to handle matters consisting of the nexus
(greatest degree prime) for all entities comprised
thereof does not present itself. Matters cannot
ascend further unless a new nexus pool is
discovered.

Principle of Trust

Each pentarchy prime degree association will review
matters that affect its pentarchy prime because of
its members' interactions pertaining to those
matters. This pentarchy prime Principle of Trust
establishes that a matter is entrusted to the
pentarchy prime that is sufficient to address all
parties involved. At the same time, there will be
certain and severely restricted number of pentarchy
prime principles that will be decreed to entrust

the sentient nexus pentarchy prime because of universally recognized application.

Assignment for Greatest Growth

The assignment of caretakers ought not to be taken lightly. The caretakers who take their positions in earnest will develop in ways that will not be apparent to them right away. This must be done selflessly. To serve others is the way to the greatest growth for an entity.

A Horrendous Feat

When one considers the pentarchy prime framework, one will recognize that the highest degree association of five (umbrella) domains will have been selected at each and every prime degree. This means that the person will have demonstrated her leadership abilities at the premiere foundation through all degrees of pentarchy primes. It is in this way that truly competent leader caretakers will be brought to the fore. This framework will ensure respect for each autonomous pentarchy prime for matters not of grave concern. More details of the process will be forthcoming as each pentarchy prime, foundation and ascension types, works them out.

Decision Appeal to Next Ascension Prime

The only time an ascension pentarchy prime will consider a matter is when one or more preceding foundation pentarchy primes issue resolutions that are considered too harsh or too extreme or violates basic pentarchy prime tenets. Otherwise, the prime directives endure with no appeal. They are enforceable and honored everywhere. For example, debts must be repaid or in good standing before new credits are forthcoming anywhere.

To Reach the Nexus

As one is selected to the next prime degree and the next until the sentient nexus is reached, one needs only to persuade or convince just five entities, oneself included, at each degree. At the fifteenth degree, the count shows that only 75 entities have to be convinced! This may appear to be a very small number. However, the feat is very great! The influences of nearly 31 billion entities were involved! The link to 31 billion entities is effectively communicated through 75 of them. Consider the notion that everyone who chooses or is able to participate is in fact part of the decision making process. They play a key role by selecting the best and most competent leader caretakers. These are all the checks and balances that are needed. Permit this system to flourish and it will be spectacular!

Pentarchy Prime Transfers

An advanced notification of a separation for a degree minus-one foundation pentarchy prime from the degree ascension pentarchy prime is permitted. Upon review of all outstanding directives and issue resolution opinions made while in the ascension pentarchy prime it is currently in, the terms and conditions is required for complete separation. The terms and conditions are reviewed by the degree plus-one ascension prime for fairness. Admittance to another ascension pentarchy prime with an available member slot is allowed after a transitional transfer period that is based on the foundation degree prime. Completion of all the directives and resolutions at the moment of the transfer request must be met. The exception is the sentient nexus pentarchy prime since there is no other ascension prime to join!

Foundation Pentarchy Prime Resolution Submissions

When a foundation pentarchy prime submits a resolution to persuade the next ascension pentarchy prime to consider, it is up to the ascension to accept the resolution and make it effective or brief the foundation why it was not accepted for inclusion. Any resolution brought to the attention of the ascension ought to be considered very seriously. This information channel is the strongest link to all umbrella pentarchy primes. This will ensure all are protected and viable.

Jurisdiction

Jurisdiction occurs at the greatest degree that encompasses all of the entities involved in an issue. Bequeathing jurisdiction on a major topic item is permitted to the next ascension pentarchy prime for a period of time, for example, five years.

Checks to Abuse of Power

There may be concern about the abuse of power by those who would preside over matters involving containment of others or other major abuses. The degree minus-one foundation pentarchy primes of five will keep them in check.

Pentarchy Prime Disappearance Scenario Action Plan

If one or more of the ascension pentarchy prime leader caretakers disappear or has been extinguished, the set of degree minus-one foundation pentarchy primes must investigate and suspend all further issue review decisions until the investigation to their disappearance is completed. The findings will be made public with full disclosures, no exceptions, at the earliest moment possible! Exceptions to early completion findings are matters that involve avoidance of grave harmful acts. They are to remain ongoing. However, interim review opinions need to be made.

The Few against the Many Monoliths

It is common practice by historical governments to view institutions as similar to themselves, as monoliths. The view is felt that governments live on and only officials are changed. When you accept this, you are expressing a belief that institutions are sound and good regardless during happenings when some of the officials are abusive in their official capacity. With this belief, it is extremely difficult for one entity to stand up to it. Many in history have been jailed, tortured, or killed. They are the ones who have grown as spiritual entities. They were able to go beyond corporeal existence and be liberated after serving time in an Earth sojourn.

Discard the monolithic institutional belief systems and accept the belief system that we will have instead caretakers or custodians who use instruments such as institutions to provide for the common good of all entities. With this framework, we do not have to make these institutions sterile or without faces. They exist to promote the decisions of society.

40

Given this, it is not to be suggested that we have to examine all workers as to proper selections. Rather, executive duty caretakers will monitor the performance and duties of all within the organization. These top caretakers can perform the duties of an aspect of societal needs. Society will issue decisions and hand the decisions to executive duty caretakers who are empowered to carry them out. Failure to perform their duties will result in dismissal and possible banishment from other similar positions in the future. Caution must be taken to ensure that decisions be selective and accommodate growth expansions of society and all its members.

Monoliths exist only at the bequest of the governed.

Misguided Finality Decisions

Historical judicial decisions were not universally applied nor were they just. They were nothing more than decisions made by feudal lords. Very restricted caring concern was applied to arrive at a final decision. Why leave important matters to anyone else than our selves? We would best be able to handle smaller manageable impact matters by the smallest pool encompassing all that are part of an issue. This way those who are closest to the events and background can make the fairest and most equitable decision.

Decision Domain

Historically, there was a fear that a judicial decision must be as complete as possible. This is absurd! Decisions can only be based on available information, understanding, and insight. Choose wise leader caretakers to make the best decisions for our times. Use "experts" when needed. They are to be viewed as instruments towards a final decision, not the definitive source for it.

To Participate in the Decision Making Process

In order to participate in the decisions of their fellow inhabitants, one must first join a group of up to four others. Discussion sessions will be conducted, which then lead to decisions for the entire group. The interference by other groups at this same degree is strictly forbidden unless grave harm has occurred or is imminent. A selected leader (thumb) is selected who speaks on their behalf and represents them to the next pool degree, comprised of four other pool leaders from their respective base pool that is comprised of five entities. The request to be in a pool can be made when a vacancy does exist. The request will not normally be refused. The only time that a person can be stripped of the privilege to participate in any pool is in the event of severe harm or killing of another entity. In this example, confinement must be served with no end date until there is a high degree of certainty that the wrongs have been replaced with repentance. A long confinement must be served by anyone committing murder. The concept of self-defense will be narrowly interpreted. When it is found to be so, no time is served, but a healing process will be strongly recommended. The other exception is when an entity has been decreed to be suspended because of serious negligence committed against another for a fixed time not to exceed the minimal term given a murderer's confinement. This entity is banished from voting at all prime degrees that the entity has been selected to participate in.

Uniform Business Laws

Business laws will be aimed at uniform agreements between entities. When very few entities find it very difficult to function within these laws, the various caretaker organizations within the umbrella pentarchy primes will intercede to return them to health. It is recognized that the most frail may have to be provided with stipends and assistance sufficient for sustenance.

Foundation Prime

Foundation Prime Degree Zero

Foundation prime degree zero, also known as universal ground, denotes each premiere sentient. Welcome!

Foundation Prime Degree One

Premiere Foundation Pentarchy Primes are identified as a prime with the designation of degree one. It is comprised of five premiere sentients. Are you one?

Entrance Agreement

All entities must sign and proclaim a Nexus Prime Association Agreement (NPAA) covering the essential guiding principles and tenets of pentarchy prime framework and its engaging spiritual developing promoting environment. Ascension primes will have more specific agreement documents as primes evolve through ascension awareness.

What is your prime designation?

Class Time

Those entities whom have expressed their intentions to join a foundation prime will be required to have an introductory class on Pentarchy Prime Foundations and then sign an agreement (NPAA) that issues are resolved through primes based on the degree-of-scope. Also, the class will cover prime directives and the importance that these directives declared will be complied with. Possible case scenarios regarding resolutions for non-compliance will be included.

Entity Choice for Premiere Foundation Pentarchy Prime

To select a premiere foundation pentarchy prime is a choice. Not to select a pentarchy prime is also a choice. In that case, a premiere foundation pentarchy prime will be chosen on an entity's behalf. Normally, it will be the final open position of five in the prime that will be chosen. This is similar to a low turnout during plurality elections in historical systems for those who do not vote. Decisions will be made on their behalf. Hence, their assigned premiere foundation pentarchy prime affiliation will be known.

Degrees of Foundation Primes

References in this guide refer to foundation primes with respect to an ascension prime. This refers to a reference degree for the five degree minus-one complement of primes that form the framework for the particular degree ascension prime.

Ascension (Umbrella) Prime

Ascensions Pentarchy Primes

In the immediate surroundings, a premier foundation pentarchy prime comprised of five entities is formed to handle matters involving said entities. This means that if there is a dispute within the group, then it is handled by the foundation prime encompassing them. The exception will be when grave bodily or mental harm will be or has been done on any entity. All other groups will not impose their decisions on the group when matters pertain only to the group. From this foundation pentarchy prime, one entity (the thumb) will be selected from the pentarchy prime to represent them at the next ascension pentarchy prime comprised of five chosen leader caretakers who represent their respective foundation pentarchy primes. This ascension (umbrella) pentarchy prime will decide on matters involving all five foundation pentarchy primes that they represent. Areas of discussion must involve matters that overlap at least two of the five foundation pentarchy primes. This process repeats to arrive at the next ascension pentarchy prime again and again until the sentient nexus pentarchy prime encompassing every entity is formed. In the context of time, this nexus formation continually expands when more nexus primes are discovered.

Umbrella Prime Governance Reach

The umbrella prime has "jurisdiction" when the Rule of Five applies. Its rules are governed and no other prime regarding business and commerce. For all other entity issues, the umbrella prime encompassing all entities for particular issue review and resolution governance applies.

Umbrella Prime Access

All leader caretakers of the degree minus-one foundation primes to a degree umbrella prime have unimpeded and unobstructed access to the first ascension prime's discussion and directive generating chambers. Access will not normally be denied to them. Exceptions are when grave harmful acts or a high degree of certainty of grave harmful acts is present.

Pent-Degree Ascension Prime

The ascension primes with degree five designation and each multiple of degree five (five times 'n' where n is any counting number) have special automatic oversight responsibilities described elsewhere. They are referred to as pent-degree ascension primes. For example, pent-degree one primes have automatic initial oversight to all pre-adult entities within their respective umbrella primes.

Completing the Pent-Complement

This rule will permit any entity to seek and find another pentarchy prime to associate with. No pentarchy prime can remain at three or fewer members for very long. Without five members, ascension cannot be made. Every effort to complete the pent-complement of five members ought to be pursued. Temporary ascension prime association is possible due to a variety of circumstances. One such circumstance is when a member has left the pentarchy prime due to member re-selection of another prime or due to natural causes. Another circumstance is when there are no more members in the degree prime pool to pursue.

Foundation Primes to Ascension Prime

The immediate five foundation primes to a particular umbrella prime will have unrestricted access to the umbrella prime and its activities.

Degrees of Ascension Primes

References in this guide refer to an ascension prime with respect to other ascension primes. This refers to a reference degree plus-one ascension prime that forms the umbrella to the five referenced degree complement of primes.

Nexus Prime

Sentient Nexus Pentarchy Prime Charter

The Sentient Nexus Pentarchy Prime Leader Caretakers (All five) have special empowerments bequeath by all primes everywhere. They are chartered to ensure a safe nexus umbrella by containing all entities that have been identified as the ones who have in great probability caused grave harmful acts or the high degree of certainty that eminent intent of grave harmful acts would have been done by them. These empowerments are of greatest importance and are given. The ultimate responsibility rests with them. There are and will be no other leader caretakers with this responsibility. Naturally, a set of great instruments comprised of nexus auspices executive officer duty caretakers whom are chartered with implementing nexus directives will be assisting in this. Checks and balances are built in for those who abuse their caretaker positions.

Nexus Prime Special Handling

Grave harmful acts or issues are reviewed by the nexus prime. The handling of all other cases is described elsewhere. There may be other empowerments bequeath by all primes in the future.

Special Governance

Nexus prime has special governance pertaining to the establishment and maintenance of universal tenets and axioms. Except for early creations, new universal tenets and axioms will be shown to be rare over time.

F. Dot

To Fill Sentient Nexus Pentarchy Prime Positions

When less than five degree minus-one foundation pentarchy primes exist at the sentient nexus pentarchy prime degree, the remaining leader caretaker positions are selected at large by all leader caretakers associated with the existing nexus degree minus-one foundation pentarchy primes.

Pentarchy Prime Set of Guiding Principles

Principle: No Ownership of Sentient Entities

There will be no ownership of sentient entities even when clones are produced.

Principle: Recognition of Pentarchy Primes

The Pentarchy Prime Model, described in more detail elsewhere, is to be the foundation for all resolutions of issues by two or more entities or associations in a sentient society.

Principle: Pentarchy Prime Right to Transfer

The right to freely transfer to any pentarchy prime is recognized provided the entity has requested admission to a pentarchy prime and the complement of five members in the pentarchy prime is not complete. New pentarchy primes can form and previously existing ones can dissolve when the need to bind by all members within a prime no longer exists. A minimal time to be defined will exist before total breakup. The method will be through advance announcement to provide sufficient time for all primes affected. The details are described elsewhere.

Principle: Reciprocal Treatment

Treat all members the same way that they themselves would like to be treated is decreed. All must adhere to the same set of tenets.

Principle: Corporeal Executions

By decree, execution of any member in captivity is
disallowed even when the member murders another
member. The basis for this is that no member is
allowed to kill another by this decree. Immediate
separation and containment will be imposed on any
member that has been determined, by whatever
avenues of resolution that exist, to have made this
gravest violation. This set of pentarchy prime
guiding principles state that no one is to be
condemned. This is especially valid when it is
later found that an incorrect decision has been
made on matters of gravest violation. If an
incorrect decision is discovered, acknowledgment of
that new decision will be made accessible to all.
This includes all files, written, oral, and other
communication mediums that exist regarding the
subject with an apology stated first.

Principle: Supreme Access to Investigative Resources

For all gravest violations, a decree exists that
places first and provides adequate resources to
resolving all murders or suspicious deaths in the
most expeditious manner possible. The tenets of the
Sentient Nexus Pentarchy Prime, which is supremely
responsible for all inquiries and determination,
have been violated. A murder matter unresolved
exists in perpetuity until a decision has been made
as to what has or may have happened to the highest
degree of satisfaction communicated by the
investigation duty caretakers assigned to the task.

Principle: Rights to One's Own Information Collected

All information collected by instruments of
Pentarchy Primes for a particular entity shall be

freely and easily accessible by this entity. The only exceptions pertain to the collecting of information in ongoing murder investigations and to protect the identities of entities who provided important information regarding murders or grave harmful actions at great risks to themselves. These at-risk entities shall be given protection assistance until threat of harm is no longer present.

Principle: Free Information towards Foundation Prime

Information passed from ascension prime to foundation prime is one of many basic tenets. Information collected by any ascension prime is to be freely available to any member within this umbrella prime. Exceptions are when information pertains to matters that if made readily available will result in a high degree of certainty that grave harmful acts will be done to entities.

Principle: Selection of at most one Premier Foundation

Each entity identified within a Sentient Nexus Pentarchy Prime domain can select or be admitted to at most one Premiere Foundation Pentarchy Prime. Willful violations can lead to the suspension of prime directive activity participation privileges for a decreed period of time.

Pentarchy Prime Potpourri of General Rights

Entity Pursuits

As societal pools declare that its members are not subjects of any nation-state, all restrictions to individual entity's or consenting entities' pursuits are lifted. Interaction restrictions are to be eliminated from all governing directives or regulations. Governing laws will only apply to all other conditions within the pentarchy primes being created. A primary consideration is in matters regarding business or the exchange of goods and services.

Shared Society Vitality

Protection against grave physical harm or in the case of children, grave psychological harm, is one of the principles of shared society vitality.

Sanctuaries for Forms of Expressions

All consenting forms of expressions will be allowed a sanctuary except for forms of violence or forced indoctrination. The sanctuary must be provided by the greatest ascension pentarchy prime encompassing all requesting the sanctuary. However, no weapons or contagion of mass destruction will be permitted.

The Rights of Groups

The need for a shared belief system to encompass numerous systems is present for the exchange of goods and services in the marketplace. The framework points to the rights of individuals and of groups. Historically, the rights of individuals were, or were supposed to be, guaranteed by various prevailing constitutions. However, the rights of groups were not guaranteed. Historical systems of justice, which are fed by the legislative process, get in the way of free association since the purpose of our system is adversarial in nature, meaning that the system pins one against another. The framework of primes provde the empowerment of two entities or groups to work out their own challenges as the first step. Only in rare situations should it be necessary to present a review and resolution referee setting when the resolution process is at an impasse. Those who agree to and identify with group associations cannot request issue resolution as separate entities. An entity has the option to withdraw from any affiliation. However, when an entity was affiliated at the time of the review petition, the resolution is binding for that entity.

The phrase 'The rights of groups' relates to the general protection right of any group of two or more entities that come together for the purpose of sharing a way of life for themselves.

Protection for Consenting Adults

Matters of private issues between consenting adults are protected from being questioned unless they pertain to gravest harmful acts issued by Sentient Nexus Pentarchy Prime. Deliberate pursuits of the truth in areas of gravest harmful acts are permitted. The truths pertaining to investigations must be forthcoming by any entity when questioned. Failure to be forthcoming may result in containment orders not to exceed five years. No tortures or forced confessions are permitted. Truths are always forthcoming in time.

F. Dot

Transfers

Entities are allowed to move from one premier foundation pentarchy prime to another after an orderly transition period. The only exception is killing or violent actions toward another. The reason is due to the violation of the supreme entity's right to bond with other entities. When violations occur, the pentarchy prime can be broken up, with each entity assigned to an available pentarchy prime.

The same rights and review evaluation process apply to ascension primes as well, with reassignment due to violations for each degree minus-one foundation pentarchy prime within the offending ascension pentarchy prime to another at the same prime degree designation.

Natural Substance Usage

By and large, no natural substance will be prohibited. Only when serious harm is present or can occur in high probability will there be limits being put in place. This also includes those situations when serious damage can be done will there be controls placed on it.

All other substances that is engineered with substantive assistance and involvement by sentient entities will these substances be regulated.

Pursuit of an Entity

A single entity's pursuits will not be regulated until they interfere with another one's pursuit. The aim for caretakers will be to illuminate a much brighter path.

Censorship

Censorship of information is supremely prohibited, i.e. summarily prohibited, unless there is a high degree of certainty that grave harmful acts are eminent should particular information be disclosed.

Entity Information Access

Non-auspices caretakers can access information regarding an entity once the particular entity whose information is being requested grants the approval.

Natural Derivatives Opinion

Unequivocal demonstration that an extracted derivative from living organism using complex extraction methods taken in moderate quantities leads to grave harmful behavior, which leads to grave harmful acts being committed, will the derivative be controlled and its use highly restricted. Otherwise, cultivation and the use of simple extraction methods will the usage of the derivative be viewed in the same way as other commonly used derivatives classified as low hazard-risk substances. Over indulgence of low hazard-risk substance by a member that leads to erratic actions leading to harmful acts to other members of society is to be viewed as a harmful member characteristics requiring member containment for safety and security reasons. Safety and security issues are everyone's concern.

Pentarchy Prime Potpourri of General Restrictions

Property Ownership

There will be a rule that no ownership of land areas or permanent structures on land is permitted. In this case, caretaking leases will be allowed when viewed as beneficial to the umbrella prime. All non-living items that can be removed relatively easily will be given the term "property" owned by an entity and passed on to another by that entity. Money accrued during one's sojourn is not included except the first twenty-five percent, a figure that can be adjusted with much discussion, whereby it can be willed to another when one's sojourn ends. A recommendation is to pass the savings on to others before departing. In this way, there is no dispute as to an entity's sincere giving.

Newly Created Sentient Form Intact

No healing practitioner will be a party to the execution of a developing sentient corporeal form while in natural or artificial incubators. It will be permitted to request premature labor for a natural incubator when grave health concerns are present. The newly created sentient corporeal form will remain whole and unharmed in these instances. Normal care of the newborn will be given in all cases. The senses—sights, smells, sounds, tastes, and touch—will come to the fore. The developing sentient corporeal forms will no longer be hidden. The life expectancy of a newborn will be based on what nature provides and not what "man-kind" dictates. We are all parties to every sojourner's journey. Each is also a party to our own. We are not separate and distinct but hold a kinship to everything around us. Our reach is as far as we are prepared and ready for.

Prime Directive Libraries

Record Keeping Charter

Record keeping systems, such as a recent conceptually recognized computer system complete with backup and disaster recovery procedures or other similar permanent recording and safeguarding instruments, will record entity foundation prime selection. There is a universally recognized tenet that puts a restriction for an entity to be "active" in only one premiere foundation pentarchy prime. This is one of the many purposes for the set of instruments known as Prime Directive Libraries.

Pent-Degree Ascension Prime Record Keeping

At each multiple pent-degree ascension prime designation starting with the first, record-keeping systems will be established and maintained within each of these umbrella primes. The nexus prime will also maintain a nexus system. The information is collected starting with the nearest pent-degree ascension prime designation from nexus prime record keeping system. Each pent-degree ascension prime record keeping system will do the same until the foundation primes are reached.

Record keeping of individual prime directives will be maintained by the respective prime. It is a requirement to archive prime directives to the nearest ascension pent-degree Prime Directive Library. This is important when ascension prime directive creation uses compliance determination to arrive at the final decree. However, the research information collection set that formed the basis for the prime directive is not required to be archived with the respective prime directive. Alternate sites to be use as backup archives would be wise to have. Only when an ascension prime directive requires the same information regarding its umbrella primes for the purpose of arriving at a decision at the ascension prime will the ascension prime retain a copy of the information.

Recording System Centers (RSC)

Prime directives or determinations will be sent to Recording System Centers (RSC) described elsewhere. These RSC will identify all entities affected by the decisions and send copies to them. For more serious violations, rapid deployment teams in close proximity to entity or entities will deliver the copies.

The primes will fund an independent service organization that is chartered to record all new or changed entity premiere foundation prime information and all prime directives. Universal entity and prime directive identifiers will be used to identify the records for easy archival and retrieval. The accuracy is to be viewed as of the highest importance possible.

Standard Fees

Standard fees will be established and revised as needed for the purpose of assessment for registering prime directives into archival registries. For those who cannot immediately handle the fees, the amount will be added to their prime account, which must be paid eventually by the prime or an ascension prime.

Special Event Recordings

Recordings of actual events will be kept for safe keeping by the qualifying ascension prime satisfying the Rule of Five test based on the members participating or as spectators in the event.

Urgent Archive of Prime Directives

It is an urgent matter to record and archive prime directives in the manner described elsewhere even in those happenings when action results will not be forthcoming in the near future due to forced compliance by pre-pentarchy prime systems. When the event occurs that highlights the eminence of pentarchy prime supremacy, all prime directives are activated if not already. Those who willfully interfere with pentarchy prime directives and activities will be subject to privilege limiting directives depending on the severity of the interference. Time will prevail in carrying out prime directives in ways that may not be apparent early on. These events will unfold in time.

Prime Supersedes

The pentarchy prime framework will supersede all pre-pentarchy prime systems. Time will make this so. The complete metamorphosis will be spectacular.

Leader Caretaker Selection

Chartered with Umbrella Prime Health

Leader caretakers have supreme responsibilities for the health of the umbrella prime they are selected to.

Role of Leader Caretaker

A role of a leader caretaker is the advocacy of wise decisions on behalf of umbrella pentarchy prime members and the resolution on issues primarily brought to their attention. On rare occasions, the issues can be recognized by observations by the leader caretakers.

Job Performances

It is not unreasonable to expect and demand that leader caretakers do what the position implies, to lead in the caretaking of primes. Members affected by their actions are the ones who will participate in evaluation of their performances.

The Selection Driving Force

Elitists are comfortable with their positions and statuses. Their primary interest is to sustain their model or framework. However, it does not include the vast majority of members in society. This then is the driving force to ensure that the selection of wise leader caretakers be promoted and to recognize that only our wise leader caretakers be supreme above all other frameworks that have been constructed or put in place to be fine tuned instruments in carrying out prime directives. Our leader caretakers will make wise decisions and be kept in check by prime memberships when decisions are no longer wise or in the best interest of the entire prime umbrella. The entire prime pool of entities effectively chooses our leader caretakers.

No Law Apron Provided

In historical view, the law is an apron to shield those in positions of responsibility from performing their duties. With pentarchy prime, leader caretakers are charted to perform these duties of responsibility. These duties are not to be taken lightly. There are no aprons to hide behind.

Responsible and Accountable

The ultimate responsible and accountable caretaking is our pentarchy prime leader caretakers. They have bequeathed access to any and all information and facilities under their umbrella. There can be no dereliction of duty or excuses. Replacement leader caretakers will be selected when this is found to be true.

Leader caretakers are empowered to gain access to all sources of the truths. This is important because it aids in arriving at the best possible prime directives.

Characteristics of a Leader Caretaker

A leader caretaker position is not for everyone. This is similar to the notion that not everyone can be an entertainer, banker, doctor, carpenter, etc. One must have the passion and the desire for it. In order to advance to the next ascension pentarchy prime, one must pass muster. Choose our leader caretakers to perform their jobs in a very positive way.

We require that caretakers may apply, not executioners!

Leader Caretakers' Duties

Leader caretakers describe vision and direction, and establish policies and mission statements for the pentarchy prime, collectively, to carry out. Auspices officer duty (career) caretakers will establish the rules and guidelines, which are to be as specific as possible and allow for effective empowerment by duty caretakers. One serves at the bequest of the pentarchy prime.

Even though a leader caretaker can choose to vary a decision for similar issues, for stability, be consistent.

Leader Caretaker Supremacy

Entity pools ought to select the wisest of leader caretakers. Leader caretakers are different from other classifications of caretakers. They have supremacy over all pentarchy prime domain activities performed by other classifications of caretakers. In this way, institutions can be dismantled when they no longer serve the entity pools that established their creations. Leader caretakers *do not* serve institutions. Institutions exist because of economy of scale, efficiency, and uniform quality in their results. They are mere instruments to carry out our decisions and pursuits for a better way of life.

A Great Honor to Serve

The greatest position that one can have in a community is that of a wise leader caretaker. Consider it your vocation. It truly is a great honor to serve!

F. Dot

Leader Caretaker Privileges

Determination of Wages

For the interim prime framework, the determination of wages will be determined by members of the particular prime and at most the five degrees of primes in the direction of foundation primes.

Leader Caretaker Review Check

Certification

The certification of a leader caretaker is the selection process. There is no school for this. Mentoring by present and previous leader caretakers may provide some insights for her.

Accountability

Our leader caretakers must account for every entity and decisions made on their behalf. They may use instruments of their own creation to assist in this.

No Passing of Responsibilities

With previous historical systems, one has to work very hard to delay making decisions for fear of falling into a legal quandary. In pentarchy primes, no legal quandary exists in arriving at wise prime directives. The responsible decision-makers are clear. No passing of responsibilities exist. When selected leader caretakers balk at resolutions, a clear provision exists to select another. Choose wisely.

Conflict of Interest Opinion

When a leader caretaker of a particular degree prime has a conflict of interest in a matter requiring a prime directive, the degree minus-one prime members that selected the leader caretaker will collectively decide on the leader caretaker's behalf. This scenario can apply to all five leader caretakers in a particular degree prime when a conflict of interest arise. This procedure only applies when at least three of the members in a particular prime in question are not themselves in a conflict-of-interest situation and these qualified members can effectively produce a prime directive.

Issue Resolution Limits

What has been described for pentarchy primes ensures that the primes remain viable. Caution must be exercised in making too many decisions, for they may severely restrict the effective resolutions by pentarchy primes at degrees towards the premiere foundation primes. Select only those urgent issues requiring decisions to be made at the next ascension pentarchy prime degree, when urgent matters are at an impasse, or that delay will severely harm another entity. At the same time, permit the selected pentarchy prime leader caretakers much maneuvering room to function. Dismiss only those who ceases to be wise leader caretakers for a variety of reasons. Set term limits after which their positions may be renewed or a better caretaker is found for the transformation time periods that follow. Finally, honor those who have served.

Actions and In-Actions

A leader caretaker will be evaluated on one's actions and also one's in-actions. An in-action speaks volumes. Listen for it.

Removal Rule

Those who abuse their positions are to be removed by the degree minus-one pentarchy prime that selected them. Four votes by this prime are needed for immediate removal for the first ascension prime. Three votes will permit advanced term ending date for the first ascension. There ought not to be any hesitation for removal and replacement of abusive leader caretakers. Built-in time limits exist on holding new selections.

De-selecting of Caretakers

In a prime, three votes (opinions) are needed to de-select an ascension leader caretaker. There is a sliding duration for position expiration as the opinion propagates through ascension primes. The newly selected leader caretaker is an advisor/consultant on matters of decisions/opinions in the current ascension leader caretaker's activities until the newly selected leader caretaker begins her term. Four votes/opinions are needed to de-select a leader caretaker at the next ascension prime immediately with a more accelerated sliding duration for further ascension primes as the opinion propagates through ascension degree primes to the Nexus Prime. The accelerated reduction duration is by a factor of five.

Pentarchy prime leader caretakers can continue to perform their non-leader caretaker duties while holding their pentarchy prime leader caretaker positions. This is valid because wise selections were made. The duration is described elsewhere.

Checks and Balances

Checks and balances are accomplished by selecting the wisest of leader caretakers, who then will keep in check the officer and executive duty caretakers in all the various areas of disciplines. Our selected wise leader caretakers will have supreme empowerments than entities not selected.

Leader Caretaker Duration

Normal Prime Determination Leader Caretaker Removal Transition Periods

Normal degree prime caretaker transitional periods are defined for a currently serving leader caretaker when three members of a particular prime at any degree designation selects a replacement leader caretaker to taker her place in serving the next ascension prime on their behalf. The currently serving leader caretaker could also be serving as a leader caretaker at a degree prime greater that the next ascension prime. The following table takes this into consideration and shows the degree prime starting with zero to be the particular prime that made the determination no matter what the actual prime degree designation in the path from premiere foundation prime to the sentient nexus pentarchy prime is. The table reflects the premise that each and every pentarchy prime can select a leader caretaker to serve on their behalf to the next ascension prime.

Selection Reference Prime Degree	Transitional Number of Earth Solar Days
0	5
1	25
2	125
3	625
4	3,125
5	3,125
Greater than 5	3,125

Urgent Prime Determination Leader Caretaker Removal Transition Periods

Urgent degree prime caretaker transitional periods are defined for a currently serving leader caretaker when at least four members of a particular prime at any degree designation selects a replacement leader caretaker to taker her place in serving the next ascension prime on their behalf. The replacement is immediate with no transitional period for the currently serving leader caretaker. The currently serving leader caretaker could also be serving as a leader caretaker at a degree prime greater that the next ascension prime. The following table takes this into consideration and shows the degree prime starting with zero to be the particular prime that made the determination no matter what the actual prime degree designation in the path from premiere foundation prime to the sentient nexus pentarchy prime is. The table reflects the premise that each and every pentarchy prime can select a leader caretaker to serve on their behalf to the next ascension prime.

Selection Reference Prime Degree	Number of Earth Solar Days
0	0
1	5
2	25
3	125
4	625
5	625
Greater than 5	625

F. Dot

Graduated Selection Scale

From premiere foundation prime to nexus prime, leader caretakers can serve a term limit from five (Nexus) to twenty five (Foundation Prime) years without the experience of a selection process event by the respective prime designation. This does not preclude a replacement selection event by members of any prime at any degree at any time. This replacement selection process is described elsewhere.

Term Limits

The sentient nexus pentarchy prime leaders will retain their positions for a period of five years before a new selection process occurs. Rotation of the selection process for an ascension pentarchy prime leader will occur in each of the five years, with one being selected in any given year. Re-selection is permitted. The duration for each preceding pentarchy prime degree can have a sliding scale towards premiere foundation pentarchy primes. This is to be determined by each ascension pentarchy prime.

Universal Prime Rule of Five

Universal Prime Rule of Five

When more than five percent of the patrons or users of environmental resources, commerce, and business governance have association with an umbrella prime outside the particular degree pentarchy prime being considered for issue review and opinion formation, then the next ascension prime is considered. This process is repeated until less than five percent of the patrons of a business establishment or venture is part of an umbrella prime. It is a given that all patrons and users can be identified to a premier foundation prime. The only exception to this is when patrons are guests or visitors because of the patrons' free choice. They would have given their consent to abide by prime directives while guests or visitors of a particular pentarchy prime. The definition of a guest is that the entity has been granted the privilege to stay for a longer period of time. When no guest status request has been made, then an entity is automatically given a visitor status instead.

An Alternate View for the Rule of Five

A different view of the Rule of Five will be given next. Both are synonymous to each other and are given to assist entities in understanding this rule using the view that can best be applied with less confusion.

Prime matters pertaining to the patrons and users of environmental resources, commerce, and business governance will be under the auspices of the nearest degree umbrella (ascension) prime closest to premiere foundation prime that encompasses greater than 95 percent of the parties (entities). Prime matters are those at the time of the issue review request. In determining the degree prime, the next degree minus-one foundation prime is considered to determine if there is not more than ninety-five percent of the parties (entities) involved at the time of the issue review request that are associated to the degree prime being considered. This process repeats until the test is satisfied. The earliest degree prime that has governance involvement when less that ninety-five percent are in the prime being considered, the immediate ascension prime is then the qualified umbrella prime for issue opinion creation.

The Rule of 95 View:

A degree umbrella prime covering at least 95% of commerce or interactions among all entities will have its governance applied. Due to entity mobility pursuits, when less that five percent of entities belong to a prime domain "outside" of the particular umbrella prime satisfying this rule, no ascension interference is permitted unless an issue violates nexus tenets and universal principles.

Environment and Commerce Consortiums - Governance Reach

Reach Review

Historically, businesses focus primarily on business interests. They will not normally consider macro (big picture) interests. However, prime leader caretakers do. All members affected are considered when issues are viewed.

The Rule of Five for Natural Environments

Issues regarding natural environment will follow the Rule of Five. Otherwise, issues involving two or more entities will be reviewed and decisions made by the greatest degree prime encompassing all involved in the issue(s).

The Rule of Five for Business and Commerce

The greatest degree ascension prime identified to produce commerce and non-violent activity guidelines is the umbrella prime where less than five percent of the pool are non-pool members affected by business and commerce.

Safety of Entities Supremacy

Business regulations and guidelines have no place when the safety interest of entities is present. It is the responsibility of leader caretakers to step in and diffuse any safety issue. Also, violence of any kind is unacceptable. In this case, rapid deployment teams will respond to this type of event.

Environment and Commerce Consortiums - Environment

The Governance Reach of Business

In regards to the reach of rules of business and commerce, it will encompass those activities where the reach is greater than ninety-five percent of the umbrella prime.

Business Patron Governance Rule

Any business that has at least ninety-five percent of its patrons (Rule of Five), including workers and employees, within a particular ascension prime umbrella will comply with the policies of said prime. This allows more degree minus-n umbrella primes, where "n" is a counting number, to have autonomy and active participation in the creation of prime directives for themselves.

Prime Governance Designation Displayed

Businesses and organizations will have prime identifiers clearly marked or displayed for prime governance. All businesses, commerce organizations, and service organizations will display and be easily accessible to all the degree prime designations whose set of business governing rules and guidelines are in effect.

Pentarchy Prime Organization Instruments

Specialized agencies charted by any designated prime will be empowered to make decisions on their own and to carry out these decisions. The designated prime has five days to decline any decision. After five days, the decision goes into affect. The prerequisite is for the agencies to forward a copy of the decision to the prime and the prime to acknowledge its receipt. Primes can not refuse receipt of the copies. Primes can choose to invalidate the decision.

Environment and Commerce Consortiums - Regulations and Guidelines

Continual Evolution

Viewed historically, business and commerce have gone through numerous "minute evolution moments". This will continue to be so in the future as well. However, the ebb and flow of prime directives will provide more timely responses.

Rules of Operation

Business will operate under the Rule of Five. Simply stated, the greatest degree ascension pentarchy prime that makes decisions and directives is chosen when the business or commerce issue affects at least ninety-five of its umbrella prime members. No other degree ascension pentarchy prime has oversight ownership when less that ninety-five percent are affected.

Equalizing Factor

For civil reviews and resolutions, an equalizing formula will be devised for allocation of resources between large business/commerce consortiums and prime members.

Business Rules of the Game

Business entities will be identified by their most ascension prime designation for the set of prime directives and companion business rules and guidelines based on the Rule of Five. All those who wish to do business in this umbrella prime must comply.

No other set applies. This premise is established for simplicity and clear identification of the rules of the game being applied.

Non-Confinement Scope

Rules and regulations pertain to non-confined members of primes not in camps or secured fortresses. Auspices executive duty caretakers are charted to formulate them.

Confinement Scope

Confined prime members have confinement governance.

Environment and Commerce Consortiums - Positions and Roles

Contact is with Executive Duty Caretakers

Unlike pre-pentarchy prime systems, institution and corporation type organizations are not the "entities" informed about prime directives in pentarchy prime framework. Executive duty caretakers are the primary entities for this information. Information includes what their roles and responsibilities are. Failure to comply can lead to their removal.

Environment and Commerce Consortiums - Fair Use Engagement Arena

Exclusion of Exclusion Clauses

Insurance will have no exclusion clauses that conflict with the purpose for the type of insurance that is being sold, for example life and wellness plans. The consumer pool will sustain any loss, or go out of business. The insurance may apply fair-use formulae to assess premiums.

Major Players

If a business consortium wants to be a big or major player in the marketplace, then a greater degree umbrella prime will be involved. All greater umbrella prime-related issues span this big or major business (player) consortium.

Rules of Engagement

The rules of engagement for business will be spelled out. More importantly, the code of conduct, which describes high qualities of conduct and aspirations, is supreme in this arena.

In the Kitchen Cooking Products

All naturally derived products from plants will have no restrictions on use and possession when cooking tools commonly found in food kitchens are used. The Rule of Five holds here in its commercial use.

"Seed Money"

For a major prime initiative, seed money in equal amounts will be given to the first twenty-five business entities that have been selected for research and development. After a pre-defined target date, a selection of five from the list will be given the go-ahead to move forward with the next phase of development and production for a period of five years. After that date, the marketplace influences will govern the outcomes. Examples of projects are new high-speed transport systems, like modern trains and tracks, for the umbrella primes.

Pentarchy Prime Termination Points

Identification of commerce distribution and services termination points is essential for clear umbrella primes business directives. It is advisable for ascension primes not to be too intrusive into more foundation prime domains. Have faith that these domains will on the whole do the right thing. Only in cases of weapons of mass destruction to include any man-made construction or mass biological contagion will ascension primes have oversight responsibilities.

Executive Duty Caretakers

Executive Duty Caretakers

This is a duty caretaker classification of caretakers that effectively oversee the vision and operation of an organization or association instrument.

Job Performance

It is not unreasonable to measure an executive duty caretaker job performance. After all, we require competent executive duty caretakers to engage in an active way.

Candidate Questionnaires

Candidates will answer questionnaires for positions as executive officer caretakers and their senior staff to learn of conflict-of-interest issues. Some examples are members of historical nation-state agencies or its official capacities. Depending on the position, the member can be disqualified and cannot serve. Reason: One cannot serve a belief system that is exclusionary in practice. Affidavits will be signed as to the truthfulness and accuracy of the responses with the knowledge that misleading and false replies may lean toward forfeitures of issue resolutions and possible exile from prime participation. The duration will start when the offending entity is effectively a part of primes by choice or when total prime sphere of influence and reach has taken hold. It must be made clear that this is a very serious offense with long period of prime directives' compliance consequence.

F. Dot

Term Limits for Executive Duty Caretakers

There are no term limits for non-auspices executive
duty caretakers. Removal is possible when there
exists a pattern of failing to comply with one or
more prime directives.

Auspices Executive Duty Caretaker

Auspices Executive Duty Caretakers

This is a duty caretaker classification of caretakers that effectively oversee the auspices of an ascension pentarchy prime instrument. She serves at the pleasure of the ascension pentarchy prime and her skills and abilities are key factors in the prime's selection.

Auspices Executive Duty Caretakers Charter

The auspices executive duty caretakers are empowered to implement prime directives assigned to them. The prime directives may be general or quite specific. When general, they are chartered with the responsibility for producing the detailed specifications and then implementing them. The umbrella prime that these caretakers serve will be provided with adequate resources to accomplish their directives.

Auspices Prime Secretary

An auspices prime secretary—a unique classification distinction among auspices executive duty caretakers—has the honor and duty of recording prime directives. Her duties include the safekeeping of the prime directives for posterity and the submission of copies of them to pent-degree archival recording centers. The requirements and procedures for these centers are described elsewhere.

F. Dot

Term Limits for Auspices Executive Duty Caretakers

There is no pre-set term limits for auspices executive duty caretakers. To be removed from this position on the opinion of the respective pentarchy prime is not to be considered an offense. To violate one's own body of rules set forth for all in the domain under her care is considered to be a more serious offense. In this case, the highest penalties and/or exclusions will be imposed for such offenses. After all, an executive duty caretaker knows what is or is not an offense and will be held to the highest standards.

Removal of Auspices Executive Duty Caretakers

Removal of an auspices executive duty caretaker holding a particular position requires three leader caretaker opinions for normal ending duration. This duration allows for a transitional period before another selected auspices executive duty caretaker to assume this position. For immediate removal requires four or more leader caretaker opinions. The latter action would normally occur for serious position violations or the failure to comply with prime directives. The umbrella prime that these caretakers serve will be provided with adequate resources to accomplish their directives.

Vocation Caretakers

Duty Caretakers (Pursuit View 1)

This is a general classification of caretakers that perform a set of duties promoting the safety and well being of other entities.

Duty Caretaker (Pursuit View 2)

The duty caretaker is a general classification for any role in a position whereby a skill is learned and performed in a job environment. Her duties, in whole or in part, provide a service or product for another member of a pentarchy prime umbrella domain.

Specialist Caretaker Professionals

The specialist caretaker professional is a general classification that includes specialists such as doctors, dentists, nurses, scientists, mathematicians, and a whole array of other classifications. Primarily, the distinction is the result of narrowing the pursuit of interest in an entity's sojourn.

Degree of Caretaking Duties

Minimum standards are required for caretaker duties.

Certification

Certification for non-leader caretaker positions must be met when defined by the umbrella prime.

Job Performances and Retention

Duty/executive caretakers will be measured on their performances and dynamic prime domain developmental needs. It will indicate whether or not to retain each distinction of classification for the purpose of certification or be de-classified.

Vocation Duty Caretaker Removals in General

Leader caretakers will make decisions in matters of removals due to serious violations by a vocation duty caretaker in any category. They will make the suggestion for the vocation duty caretaker to resign before a more drastic opinion is issued to remove the caretaker from her position with serious consequences. Serious consequences can include the added provision that no holding of the same or similar caretaker positions from five up to twenty-five years depending on severity of the offense or refusal to step down.

The objective is to get the duty caretaker to leave her position in the most expeditious manner when the duty caretakers in charge failed to follow prime directives.

Non-Compliant Caretaker

The objective regarding the general classification of caretakers who violate prime directives is to remove them from positions and related privileges. Fines can be fixed amounts or be a percentage of an assessment. Usage of a fixed percentage will be found to be more equitable for all those who are in serious violations. Fines are best for minor offenses.

Sabbatical Decree

The sabbatical decree duration from holding a position once a decision is made for an entity's removal will commence five days after stepping down. This decree is specified in a prime directive or an auspices executive duty caretaker's directive.

Natural Environment-Based Caretakers

Natural environment-based caretakers will be registered with the umbrella prime based on the Rule of Five. Support packages are provided when their missions are for the greater good of the umbrella prime. It may be necessary to rotate all whom desire to participate when resources are fixed in amount. Natural environment-based executive caretakers will be identified to hold these long-term positions. They will be selected based on their skills and abilities matching the positions' qualifications.

Officer Duty Caretakers Responsibilities

Leader caretakers selected by particular pentarchy primes do not normally establish the detail rules or the monitoring of daily activities. They appoint executive officer duty caretakers to carry out responsibilities for the care of the general public. Removal of an executive officer duty caretaker is done with four out of five leader caretaker opinions of the pentarchy prime umbrella. Otherwise, the same rules set forth by executive officer duty caretakers are to be followed by everyone under the umbrella. For demonstration of support, umbrella prime leader caretakers are included with the rule set compliance.

F. Dot

Access to Information

Duty caretakers will keep no information secret when the information serves a vital public interest or the well being of all. All information will be available to leader caretakers without restrictions. Failure by knowingly withholding essential information by duty caretakers is a serious offense that will normally lead to immediate removal of caretaker duties and restrictions on similar positions in the future.

Review and Remedy Duty Caretakers

This is a classification of caretakers, historically known as court judges, to preside in matters that require review and resolution activities for disputed issues brought to the Auspices Review and Remedy Instruments by members of the community. These issues are not to be of the most serious kind, which are specifically the responsibilities of the sentient nexus pentarchy prime and auspices instruments.

Pre-Adult and Adult Sponsor Caretakers

Sponsor Caretakers

This is a general classification whereby as sponsor caretakers of an entity, they will collectively participate in the caretaking decisions involving the entity. There will be no tolerance for selection determination confrontations. When primary determination confrontations ensue, those sponsor caretakers involved will be temporarily removed from sponsor caretaker status. Those sponsors remaining will be allowed to continue their responsibilities. With temporary sponsor removal status, those who show sincere effort to be viable sponsor caretakers once again will be allowed back in the caretaking activities of an entity. Sponsor caretakers are to be viewed as providing the best form of caretaking.

Pre-Adult Sponsor Caretaker

Pre-adult members will have oversight sponsor caretakers to assist them in their adult-maturing development. The pre-adult sponsor caretakers are normally first assigned to parental entities unless relinquished by parents or when there is a high certainty that grave safety or developmental harm is imminent.

Those who are sponsor caretakers for a pre-adult will have the designation removed when harm is done or the potential for grave harm is imminent. No more than five primary or principal caretakers are assigned per child.

Until they reach or are declared adult-status entities, children who have serious issues pertaining to them are to be reviewed by the first pent-degree ascension prime. Prime of degree five is another name for the same designation. This is based on the parents/custodians who are their caretakers.

The guidelines above apply when sponsor caretakers are available. In cases when none are available, please be the one to step in when a void is there. If you step in during emergency situations when they occur, your sincere attempts will not be viewed as prejudicial. Thanks go to all ahead of time.

Default Ascension Prime Pre-Adult Oversight

Pent-degree ascension primes automatically oversee the care of pre-adult within the umbrella prime unless specific expanding degree ascension prime decisions override due to harmful environments that were not being addressed by the pent-degree ascension primes. This issue ought to be rare.

Five Year Term Minimum

Pre-adult caretakers will be specifically identified for five-year terms. Those who do participate in caretaker duties will normally be renewed.

Guardian Auspices

Pre-adult members (children) are automatically under the auspices of the first pent-degree pentarchy prime for matters pertaining to guardian oversights. No child will be invisible to this degree pentarchy prime. It is one of their primary responsibilities in making this so. Reviews are made at this designation for identification and re-establishing of pre-adult sponsor caretaker designation. Recommendation for child-care events ought to be followed. Removal of designation when recent child endangerment events have been found to be true or imminent child endangerment is very probable and ever present.

Pre-Adult Support Payments

Dependent support when decreed will not be greater than what is given as universal dependent deduction purposes. The first pent-degree prime will make that determination. Even for entities of limited resources, amounts are the same and owed over time to ease the burden.

Custody is not the Issue

The aim as it pertains to a child is not to decide who has custody, which is a historical entity property term, but rather who will be members in a group of caretakers for the child in all growth developmental matters pertaining to the child.

Automatic Sponsor Caretaker Assignments

Children will automatically have pre-adult sponsor caretakers assigned when natural adult family members are not available. These sponsor caretakers may not be perfect ones but will be ones who have the passion to do the best job they can. Only when serious harm is possible or has been done will the position be taken away. It is important to keep in mind that we are all growing. Sincere caretaking efforts are to be recognized and applauded.

High Priority Assignment

A very high priority for identifying child development caretakers (Pre-adult sponsor caretakers) is ever present whenever a child is without one. The fist pent-degree pentarchy prime will be primarily responsible for its oversight. The assignment will always be for a child development caretaker. Urgent caretaking organization instruments may be needed for very short stays. "Big sisters and brothers" are asked to apply. You are welcomed.

Adult Designation

Bequeathing of an adult designation of an entity is made by the nexus pentarchy prime or the first pent-degree pentarchy prime, whichever is closest to premiere foundation prime degree. This can be declared by an automatic age attainment directive or due to a prime determination request by an entity in question and subsequent opinion concurrence.

The nexus pentarchy prime will establish the maximum adult attainment age for all entities able to make effective sentient decisions of their own. The degree of effective sentient decision creation determination will be defined to encompass close to one hundred percent of members within the nexus prime.

Adult Sponsor Caretakers

When an adult entity is not able to respond because of medical or bodily impairment, those who have personal involvement will decide on the entity's behalf. When a dispute arises that challenges a right of sponsorship, the earliest degree umbrella pentarchy prime encompassing all parties will select the sponsor caretakers. If, however, a sponsor caretaker is determined to have a very minor involvement or none at all, the degree prime that initially review the matter can defer a decision to the degree minus-one foundation pentarchy prime encompassing the smaller umbrella prime.

When no adult sponsor caretakers are present, the premier foundation pentarchy prime is initially given the responsibility for the decision. When no adult sponsor caretaker is available and viable, the next ascension pentarchy prime will be responsible for the decision. This repeats until the pent-degree pentarchy prime is found. Load balancing spanning a greater degree than pent-degree umbrella prime may be needed on occasions when major catastrophic events do occur.

Only interested entities who were/are involved with the well being of another entity are to be the primary ones who have the particular entity's best interest in mind and spirit. An auspices instrument will not have ultimate decision over the welfare of the entity unless no sponsor caretakers have come forward with their declarations. Every effort will be made to have the entity's stay short.

Pentarchy Prime Associations

Initial Prime Framework Construction Associations

Five years will be the minimum membership association declaration with their respective foundation pentarchy primes before making another selection. It is important to choose carefully because of this long-term commitment during the early years of pentarchy prime framework construction. The aim in the beginning is to learn from our experiences in the turnaround of wise decisions formed in a shorter time. After this birth and early growth period, a minimum of twenty-five days from declaration signing is given before making another selection. After this minimum period, the entity is viewed as being a permanent member.

The reader may view the above guidelines as promoting a volatile environment. In time, it will be learned that it is more important to an entity to participate with their encounters in arriving at their own prime directives. The above guidelines provide escape clauses when prime associations become unbearable.

Single Domain Association Identification

Any entity can declare and be admitted into our pentarchy prime environment from a non-pentarchy prime environment. When this happens, identification for any non-pentarchy prime association domain is not recognized. Should an entity make a request to retain her prior identification, no pentarchy prime association is allowed and restricted visitors routes and sites are permitted only. Violations result in banishment from umbrella prime domains.

Change in Foundation Prime

Entity move requests to another premiere foundation prime are normally granted. There is a twenty-five day limitation on issues from initial notification before a different umbrella prime can review any issue regarding the entity. A twenty-five day to five year sliding scale is used as entity issue is reviewed at each step-degree umbrella prime to the nexus prime.

Prime Association Identification

A nexus universal symbol will define each pentarchy prime degree jurisdiction. A second uniquely designed symbol can be adopted by each prime of their own choosing to represent their distinctive prime identity.

Prime Designation

What is your prime designation?

Choice of Foundation Prime

All entities that are not confined can choose the premiere foundation prime of choice. Matters involving two or more members within an umbrella prime can defer the final opinion (decision) to a degree minus-n foundation prime that also is the umbrella prime to all parties. The view is that the opinion (decision) that the matter can best be handled is at the more inclusive prime. An example may be due to the close proximity of the matter (issue) with the prime identified. Examples are commerce, vehicle traffic patterns, air flights, sporting events, local sanitation services, etc. A partial decision may be rendered by the greatest ascension prime with the complement portions of the final decision deferred to an umbrella degree prime closer to premiere foundation prime.

Default Foundation Prime Selection

Foundation prime selection guidelines are imposed and enforced when an entity cannot decide her foundation prime identity. In this case, the designation prime that is determined is based on the interactions of other entities of the pent-degree prime regarding the entity in question and by the Rule of Five. Should this scenario not be easily determined, then the pent-degree prime with members in close proximity of the entity based on the Rule of Five will select on her behalf. Additional guidelines regarding more specific scenarios will be described in greater details at a later date.

Consider Rapid Turnaround Selection

One can consider proximity of prime members when joining a foundation prime. Also for prime leader caretaker, the same is true for ascension prime. This suggestion is not an absolute. However, rapid turnaround can be achieved more readily in prime review and directive activities.

Prime Separation Events

When pentarchy primes are separated due to natural barriers that are beyond control of the primes, temporary inclusive domain systems are formed in order to continue caretaking responsibilities until cohesive links with the others are restored. This means the establishment of a new premiere to nexus pentarchy prime framework.

Registration Research

Entity requests for foundation prime registration can select a characteristic category type for prime selection. A list of the primes and their affinity types are compiled and provided for selection determination. Archival Auspices Libraries are entrusted with this responsibility.

Consider a Viable Selection

In considering affinity type premiere foundation prime versus geographic positional foundation prime selection, the former will demonstrate its superior viability over time.

Registration of Visitors

During transformation and beyond, those who wish to visit or immigrate must register and declare their intentions. Once the immigration intent is registered and it is to immigrate, then they are given the chance to select premiere foundation pentarchy prime or are automatically assigned to one. In the latter case and once readjustment is complete, selection of a particular prime is allowed.

Pentarchy Primes Supersedes

In joining a prime, affirmation is made that decisions made by the prime in matters involving two or more member entities will be followed. All other decision-making systems do not supersede systems of pentarchy primes.

Pentarchy Prime Environment

Terrorist Regimes Identified

The policy of non-entry of entities into a domain defines it as a terrorist one as viewed by those who are excluded. In fact, this view will be shown to be universal. It will be so that terrorist regime will be dismantled wherever they may occur.

Non-Citizen Criminal Intent

No law or tenet will exist that defines sentient beings as being criminal because of being non-citizen. All non-harming sentient entities will have safe passage throughout primes' public passage routes.

Safe Passage

No entity can be considered a criminal for wanting to be free by entering a geographic boundary. A primary purpose of pentarchy prime is to ensure safe passage for all entities who travel throughout it.

All primes will allow safe passage through their primes for any entity. Exception for passage is when entity is confined for grave harmful acts.

Favorable Conditions

There is not to be condemnation so that conditions can be favorable for minimal or non cover-up on the true nature of the problem. The aim is to rectify harmful conditions quickly so that favorable conditions are restored.

Active Participation

Review your primes at all degrees and offer recommendations for improvements. You will find that the vast majority of leader caretakers welcome this.

Entity Information Access

Freedom to access any information on one's self is normally granted, except when murder or grave harmful acts have occurred and the investigations are ongoing.

Privileges Restored

When an entity's probation period is complete due to the serious nature of the violation or offenses, all privileges are to be restored unless specifically noted in the review directive.

Parallel Family Household Preserved

Pentarchy prime framework recognizes a family unit consisting of parents or pre-adult sponsor caretakers and children. This framework will not treat members poorly. To aid every member's basic viability needs will be explored and implemented. To help another will lead to the same being reciprocated.

Children's care will be under the auspices of the first pent-degree umbrella prime as the primary pentarchy prime for review checks in favorable developmental environments. This umbrella prime has the first responsibility to intercede when harmful environments exist.

Urgent Charitable Work

When urgent charitable work is being carried out, obstacles will be removed by temporarily lessening the codes and standards that exist until the urgency has passed, at which time the higher codes and standards are restored.

Modes of Movement

A key success factor for pentarchy primes is to have various modes of transportation and access routes. There must be viability for all modes and not be limited to one or two primary modes. Alternatives ought to be pursued so that they can be accessible to all by using one of many modes.

Venues of Entity Pursuits

Good faith attempts will be made for specifying conditions that satisfy entity or entity group requests to perform pursuit ideas. Exceptions that prohibit them are when there is a high certainty that grave harm would be experienced by other entities.

Pentarchy Prime Governance

Leader caretakers oversee ALL

Historically, a government based on a nation-state framework is nothing more than having the elite in positions as land-based lords. Wars are started to secure and maintain artificial boundaries or fences. Leader caretakers do not require borders to wisely lead the pool that selected them.

General Reach

Historically, the legal system defined and handled matters that pertain to properties and their holdings of them. Entities are not to be viewed as property but rather are to be viewed in the well being and protection of primes. It is up to wise leader caretakers when entities may pose a danger to other entities and their well being and protection.

Minimum of Two

Primes deals with matters involving two or more members in their respective primes. For matters involving a singular member, that singular member handles them. Respect this.

Nation-State Jurisdiction

Nation-states have no jurisdiction over other nation-states. Only ascension pentarchy primes do.

F. Dot

Evenly Spread

In historical legislative, judicial, and executive (triad) societal framework, massive laws and regulations must be passed, administered, and judged by few officials who preside over their application. With pentarchy prime, the decisions are spread more evenly and are more effective because matters are resolved at the optimum degree prime that spans all members and no greater!

Premier Prime Directives

When no rules and regulations exist to address an issue by two or more members of an umbrella prime, then the responsibility for their creation is the domain of the leader caretakers of the umbrella prime. Initially, they may be general in scope and application. Time may be needed for wise refinements. The wise usage of "time" applies here.

Geographic and Environmental Domains

Geographic and environmental domains are preserved under the auspices of umbrella primes based on the "Rule of Five" described elsewhere. Exceptions for non-preservation and non-sustaining activities can only be considered when an ongoing plague is present or a real possibility. In this case, a greater degree prime may recognize the situation to be of grave concern and intercede for the well being of all.

Bequeathing Caretaking to the Next Degree

Jurisdiction occurs at the umbrella degree prime that effectively encompasses all parties in an issue. Bequeathing jurisdiction on a subject matter can be made to the next ascension degree for a period of five years.

Access to Information

There will be no restrictions on an entity's own information recorded anywhere. Access to public information, which is maintained by any particular pentarchy prime, will be made available to all within the pentarchy prime umbrella. Those who administered treatments, for example doctors, will be regulated that describes the information to be collected and stored.

Revenue Sharing

Any resources, historically referred to as "revenue", collected by ascension primes are to be shared by the umbrella foundation primes. The shared resources allocation is based on wise usage and need.

Environmental Stewardship

Leader caretakers will, after much consultation with advisory duty caretakers, identify land, sea, air, space zones, etc. that can be given temporary stewardship for business, foundation prime, and/or entity usage. All usage code standards for its use must be complied with for continuous privilege usage.

Professional Certification Boards

Establish monitoring and evaluation auspices boards for the professional duty caretakers. The auspices will provide performance qualification ratings to aid any entity's need for such information.

A Primary Mission Statement

A primary mission statement of pentarchy primes is the identification and promotion of caretakers in their wise caretaking of entities in their domains. Historically, systems of laws in micromanaging behaviors maintained the premise that no uniqueness exists. Everyone and everything is identical in its application. This is a false premise. Diversity exists and is universal. Embrace it; promote it; allow for variances to exist! Wise decisions are welcomed. However, it would be wise to be uniform when common elements or application threads exist.

Final Decree

Leader caretakers are the final arbiters in all matters involving their umbrella primes, inclusive. As described elsewhere in this guidebook, rely on the Rule of Five for matters pertaining to usage of natural resources, businesses, and commerce regarding efficiencies and to prevent review and resolution matters from going to a halt. Do establish auspice agencies to be instruments of pentarchy primes, where appropriate, to handle routine or common matters not pertaining to unique urgent consequence issues to the general umbrella primes. Our respective pentarchy prime leader caretakers will etch well-formed principles and guidelines to assist us in our pursuits.

Ownership of Information

Information produced or collected in a pentarchy prime is to be shared by all entities within its umbrella. The referenced pentarchy prime may be required to share it with other pentarchy primes at the same prime degree. Here is how it works. A foundation pentarchy prime can produce or collect information to be shared within its pentarchy prime umbrella. However, the next ascension pentarchy prime must decide to collect the same type of information before it can be shared with its umbrella primes. This constitutes the right to privacy and related matters.

Bequeathing Decision Review and Resolution Domain Review

Decisions are to be made at the earliest foundation degree prime whenever possible. Jurisdiction is to be respected and resolutions honored with no exception except as explicitly expressed elsewhere, because of the serious nature of the issue review item. Decisions can be delegated to the next ascension pentarchy prime when review and determination requests are made by the foundation prime. The resulting decision by the ascension prime with sufficient opinions by leader caretakers is then binding. A request for insight can also be requested. The opinion may be used in arriving at a decision for the foundation pentarchy prime decision. In both situations, a fee may be permissible. The criterion for a particular pentarchy prime to have responsibility for a decision is when an issue impacts two to five of the foundation pentarchy primes within the prime.

Collection Set of Information

Information collected within a pentarchy prime umbrella remains within it unless a prime directive by the umbrella prime is made releasing the information to the ascension prime. This rule does not apply when the ascension prime is also collecting similar information by all degree minus-one member primes.

Ascension Prime Serious Issue Review

It will be one of the primary missions for primes to uncover the truth in matters that are of the serious nature initiated by more foundation primes when matters are not brought to ascension primes for a variety of reasons. The final onerous is on applying wise usage of prime activity avenues.

Umbrella Prime Re-sizing

When entities from other primes have affected non-environment and commerce consortium actions by a more foundation degree umbrella prime and its members, then the umbrella prime encompassing the tighter degree will be involved.

Pentarchy Prime Governance Instruments

A Lease Arrangement

With pentarchy prime framework, there is no propensity for war over land. The need to guard boundaries is non-existent. Besides, what would you defend? Land is a caretaker lease arrangement with the umbrella primes affected. The wise usage of land is promoted by primes. Hoarding is not allowed. Feudal lords need not apply.

The Service of Institutions

Pentarchy prime framework requires leader caretakers take charge and make wise decisions. Leader caretakers do not serve institutions. Institutions, hereafter known as Pentarchy Prime Instruments, exist when prime directives warrant them.

Composition of Juries

Returning to the notion of an integrated system of justice, a more involved community participation in a just system will be found to be superior. For matters not pertaining to the highest degree of urgency, a panel of five jurors, two selected from one party's pool of peers, two selected from the other party's pool of peers, and one from the professional jurist pool, will preside in deciding the outcome of a non-harmful matter. This framework instrument is being proposed as an interim one or a long term one should leader caretakers choose it to be so to handle issues and matters not pertaining to present or future grave harmful acts. The earliest degree foundation prime that encompasses all the parties in an issue or matter defines the jurist selection pool. All parties may make any comment of their choosing, which has a bearing on the issue or matter, without censorship. A time limit may be imposed on each member who testifies so that it speeds up the process when needed. The goal of the proceedings is to be just and fair without the tone of condemning or victimizing. The aim should always be to deny privileges when a violation has been done, to recover loss of possessions by the violator, or to assist in the healing process when it is recognized that the assistant approach will have a long term lasting benefit to the whole. Confinement camps are cruel and are used as a last resort for blatant or habitual violations. An entity should be held when the entity flees from the scene of a harmful event like, for example, a serious accident, without first being released by a recorder-of-events officer duty caretaker on the scene.

Auspices of Pentarchy Primes

Instruments responsible for rules and guidelines based on prime directives exist under the auspices of pentarchy primes.

Long Standing Instrument Organizations

The instrument organizations established by primes will certify professional ranks that are especially involved with the health, welfare, and security of its members. It is the responsibility of these same prime instrument organizations to review each certification on a periodic basis and when grave harm has been done or have a high degree of certainty of happening. The respective umbrella prime is liable for offenses when early warning signs were ignored.

No Second Guessing

Leader caretakers will not second-guess business decisions. However, rules and regulations on conduct and fairness will be established. Those particular rules and regulations that have high prime importance designation will be monitored by instrument auspices of the primes. Removals of business executives are based on these high prime designations.

Pentarchy Prime Instrument Review Period

The leader caretakers of a particular pentarchy prime have five days to void proposed standards and guidelines produced by auspices executive caretakers of the prime auspices instruments. Opinion review feedback by leader caretakers can assist in rapid refinements when proposals are voided. In general emergency and when decrees are not related, the time for rejection is twenty-five days. These auspices prime instruments are chartered with implementing guiding principles created by leader caretakers' prime directives.

Identification Access Speed Instrument

There is no need for bar codes on entities, since every entity is a member of at most one premier foundation prime. All ascension primes are derived from foundation primes that every entity can eventually be identified. However, an identification access speed instrument can be used to greatly speed up admission or perform transactions to primes' societal activities.

Pentarchy Prime Issue Formation

Prime Directive

A prime directive is the outcome of issue review and discussion activities by a particular pentarchy prime. This is due to an issue involving matters that pertain to two or more of its members. The prime directive reflects on the issue and specifies the resolution regarding it.

Candidate Issues

Candidate issues for prime decisions are based on the high probability that interactions of entities exist.

Size the Issue

The "size" of an issue is reviewed first. Then the review and resultant opinion of the issue is made at the correct "degree-size" pentarchy prime based on the issue's reach.

No Issue Delays

A prime has five days to validate an issue involving two or more members are in fact within their respective umbrella prime jurisdiction. Otherwise, the next ascension prime is involved in the issue unless the ascension prime cannot validate within five days. This process continues until an umbrella prime is found. This rule illustrates the importance of prime members' record keeping caretaking and preservation.

Types of Issues

Primarily, leader caretakers will be involved with types of issues that have not been addressed before. Established prime directives that are in existence at the present will govern normal or routine issues.

Matters brought to the Fore

Pentarchy primes deals with matters not specified anywhere else as rules and guidelines that were implemented or previously defined prime directives.

New Issues

All existing prime directives must be in compliance before new issues raised by a prime member can be considered and handled by the prime's leader caretakers. To be in compliance can mean a scheduled action as set forth by prime directive(s). Exceptions are when matters pertain to grave harm that has been committed or there is a high degree of certainty that grave harm will be committed by the member.

Towards Ascension Prime

By registering your prime directives, future resolution petitions will more effectively review available information in rendering a newly created wise prime directive. These early directives set the stage for future directives at all degrees. All opinions do count.

Pentarchy Prime Issue Discourse

Review Delays

When an entity or leader caretaker requests review of an issue, the review will happen when all prime directives are complete or are making satisfactory progress towards their completion. The delays are then due to and rests with the entity making the request. Exceptions are when grave emergencies exist.

Filibuster

A filibuster in prime terms means to withhold one's decision. Other leader caretakers within a prime can move forward with a final directive when sufficient opinion votes are present. Two filibusters can delay a permanent prime directive. Should the non-filibuster members provide the three sufficient opinion votes for a resultant prime directive, the prime directive is temporary for twenty-five days. The prime directive creation impasse will need to secure sufficient opinion votes to continue the same prime directive another twenty-five days. This is repeated whenever two leader caretakers in a prime choose to filibuster. Otherwise, the prime directive is permanent. When this filibuster situation event does occur, this type of event ought to alert members within an umbrella prime to take notice and get involved in assisting the resolution of this impasse. The assistance may lead to the selection of a replacement of one or more leader caretakers.

Pentarchy Prime Issue Resolution

Initial Pentarchy Prime Issue Requester

When a prime decision has been made and passed on to members within the prime who had the issue initially presented to the prime, the members must abide by it. Failure to comply by any member will cause suspension of further consideration for any current and future issue review requests brought by the non-compliant member.

NOTE: Consider using arbiters in pentarchy primes doctrines everywhere.

Interim Consuls

We will have interim consuls and arbiters to handle the transitional judicial reviews. Prime tenets are supreme and the consuls and arbiters will ensure that these tenets are not violated when reviewing historical references.

Leader Caretaker Opinions

For any prime, three yes opinions are needed for a decision to have creditable prime directive status recognition. In time of emergencies, one leader caretaker of the five in a prime is needed for a temporary decision to be carried out. Within 25 hours, the complement of the three minimum decisions is needed to remove a temporary decision to be longer term. Contingencies may need to be considered, which is why these temporary measures are needed. These events ought to be rare.

Text Available to All

The text to all prime decisions will be made available to all entities within the umbrella prime. The exceptions will be when there is a high probability that should a decision be made readily available, there is a high degree of certainty that grave harm may be committed by those who are viewed as violent entities and are not presently in containment.

A Procedure for Issue Review Escalation

For review escalation for non-harmful originating prime directive, the complainant must leave the foundation pentarchy prime for another. This will encompasses a greater ascension pentarchy prime before the initial complaint request can be considered by the greater ascension pentarchy prime. An example of this is the following. A traditionally married couple in the same umbrella prime must "de-couple" before escalation reviews can be considered in regards to complaints between the marriage bound entities. The respecting of pentarchy primes is normally given except for those provisions already spelled out elsewhere regarding grave offenses.

Record Keeping

An information system will be developed and maintained to keep track of all associations. Access to it is to be easily acquired by any member within the umbrella prime. Any matter involving two or more pentarchy primes at the same prime degree will be resolved by the immediate ascension pentarchy prime encompassing all. A pentarchy prime session will convene as needed.

Source of Resolution Insights

Reviewing member foundation primes' prime directives by umbrella prime members does provide good insights regarding the health and wise decision making activities of the more foundation primes. Umbrella prime can determine when assistance is urgently needed. Look there first.

The Rule of Five Review and Resolution Ceiling

On occasions, there may be appeals to the next ascension prime to determine if a particular prime directive is viewed as harsh. If so, a review is stated with comment and passed to foundation prime or petitioner requesting this review. A modified prime directive may be produced. This process repeats until five degrees of ascensions have been contacted. Review and resolution can yield a neutral outcome. It this case, the original prime directive is left as-is.

Interim Directives

Some issues can be deferred when the subject matter requires more thought and discovery. In those cases, an interim directive will be issued and have a preface stating that this directive is interim in scope and that the issue may be re-visited at a later time after additional thought and discovery activities.

Pentarchy Prime Issue Resolution Implementation

Clarification Prime Directive Expansion

Prime directive refinements are needed only to clarify decision-making directives when the executive duty caretakers are unsure how to resolve an issue or when leader caretakers think the issue is of a greater importance to require a wise refinement.

Language of Choice

Dissemination of information and prime directives will be made using the language of choice selected by each pentarchy prime that issued them. One or more languages may be chosen.

Prime Directives Courier System

A separate auspices courier system will exist to communicate prime directives to all foundation primes within umbrella primes.

Archival Prime Directives

Permanent archival backups of prime directives are required. The activities and specifications are described elsewhere.

Further Classifications

Primes define the terms and conditions. Auspices executive duty caretakers will identify the items, properties, entities that are impacted by those terms and conditions.

Leader Caretaker Executor Refusal Requests

If a leader caretaker is selected to be the champion for the implementation of prime directives finds it difficult to execute a decision by the prime's group of leader caretakers because of strong beliefs, she may request that it be re-assigned to another, one who has decided with the majority. This request will normally be honored.

Auspices of Arbiter Caretakers

Actions and decisions by caretakers are based on prime directives where applicable. When excerpts become the norm through implementation, they become codified and under the auspices of arbiter caretakers. The arbiter caretakers will preside over issue review and resolution outcome within their auspices.

Member Restriction Database

Primes will maintain databases pertaining to privileges of entities that have been granted or restricted based on prime directives. A list of generalized categories will be used to identify privileges. An example is vehicle usage, public transportation (air, bus, train, shuttle, etc.), retail shopping, etc. Failure to comply with restricted privileges will result in being restricted to containment camps.

Umbrella Prime Foundation Allocations

Allocations of monetary instruments will normally be equally distributed to the umbrella foundation primes. To have unequal distribution of money allocations is when all five prime leader caretakers choose otherwise. An example is when a natural catastrophe has occurred and the passion to help out exists in this situation.

Most Favorable Displacement Options Status

There will be events when decisions require the closure to a way of life for an entity or a group of entities due to serious safety and health issues or due to a major shift in direction for the vibrant development of the greater umbrella prime. When this happens, then the entity or group will be given Most Favorable Displacement Assistant Options (MFDAO). These MFDAO are the same ones that are granted to anyone within the umbrella prime decreed by umbrella prime directives.

It is Imperative!

It is imperative that all prime directives be satisfied and carried out.

Pentarchy Prime Remedies for Failure of Implementation

Credit Worthiness

Transformation to the nexus is by way of decisions and the recording thereof. Failure of an entity to follow through on decisions from the primes will lead to suspensions of "credit worthiness status" of the entity in all future decisions involving entity. A specified duration after the entity complies is used to return the entity to "credit worthiness status" once again. This duration depends on the severity of non-compliance issue.

High Contractual Risk Entities

Those entities that fail to comply with prime directives after a reasonable period of specified time will be identified as "high contractual risk entities" in the respective umbrella prime issuing the alert. This may have the affect of rendering all future contractual agreements with other entities within the prime as having no value and will not be recognized by the prime.

Violation Review Consideration

No violations of prime directives are acceptable, lest they are in conflict with ascension prime directives or basic tenets. When there is a conflict, then the ascension primes may review foundation prime directives and render decisions when called into questioned as they pertain to ascension prime directives.

Longevity of Non-Compliance

An entity habitual failure to comply with prime directives will lead to the suspension of future issue review and resolution regarding the entity until all current directives have been complied. This identification will be made public so as to alert other entities that review and resolution for issues involving this particular entity will normally be at risk.

Warning: Serious Violation

Failure to comply with prime directives is a very serious violation. The warning will be disseminated throughout the prime.

Statute of Limitations

Statute of time limitations will exist so that performances of executive and duty caretakers can be measured. Pass the time statue limits and all information is available to anyone in the prime who requests it. Examples are murders, child endangerment, and child disadvantage action results.

Suspension of Review

The failure of one of five leader caretakers in a pentarchy prime and her umbrella primes to comply with a decision made by the other four will be to suspend all further items that may be reviewed regarding issues originating from her umbrella primes for consideration. This will result in the halt to decisions rendered pertaining to matters of the foundation pentarchy prime represented by the one leader caretaker who refused to complied with one or more prime directives.

The failure of two of five leader caretakers in a pentarchy prime and their foundation primes to comply with a decision made by the other three will be to suspend all further items being reviewed from any foundation prime to the umbrella prime. A way to resolve this impasse is of the highest priority and ought to be found with the greatest earnestness.

An exception to the above can be made as it pertains to natural disasters or grave emergencies.

Non-Threatening versus Threatening Issues

An Offensive Event Defined

An offensive event has occurred when harm is done through the eyes of the victim and not those of the observers. All parties involved must work out fair resolution of the event. Exceptions are pre-adults and those who cannot articulate their perspectives. Compassion and understanding are the guiding forces in such matters. Recognition that every entity is developing at her level and pace will be recognized and adequate assistance provided when possible. A measured response is to be taken for the offense. No excessive response is allowed. It may be as routine as to issue an order for the entity that is viewed as harmful to keep away from the entity that feels threatened.

Universal Violation

The ultimate act considered a violation of all is that which is of grave importance to all. It is the extinguishing of corporeal life of another member. The reason is that this act prevents the free association to any sect in the entire nexus prime.

Temporary Separations

There are times that some entities cannot function well due to not having sufficient preparations to make it so. In these cases, it may require separations from the general population so as not to bring grave harm to others. These separations, which are confined to camps with others of similar challenges, are to be as short as possible. All possible adequate preparation caretaking ought to be explored.

Far Less Than Grave Offenses

When less than grave offense discoveries have been made and identified by auspices overseers, the leader caretakers representing the pentarchy prime umbrella have up to 125 days to charge the offenders and up to another 125 days to render a decision. This time duration is codified for performance evaluation activities and the pool members' early access to all information. The proceedings and decisions can be delegated to a decision-making body with appointees. This decision-making body can be a standing one with appointees appointed for fixed time duration.

Privilege Removal and Duration

As it pertains to violation resolution, the time limit ban for specific areas of activities or privileges must be spelled out in decisions. Total activities will not be banned unless maximum-security containment orders resulting in confinement were issued as part of the resolution order. Minimum basic needs are not to be denied.

Less Than Extreme

For more serious offenses other than extreme violent offenses, the next ascension prime will intercede to handle evaluation and remedy an opinion.

Suspension of privileges

For offenses not involving harmful acts to others, entities violating pentarchy prime decisions will have privileges suspended for a period of time. Repeated suspensions will yield longer privileges suspension time periods. Exile from the pentarchy prime may be a final resolution for habitual violations. Admission to another pentarchy prime is permitted after 125 days or multiples of 125 days, depending on the severity of the violation in the current umbrella pentarchy prime. The next ascension pentarchy prime will decide in these matters unless it is the nexus pentarchy prime already.

Time Limits on Charges

Only entities that commit murder (the deliberate extinguishing of life) can have up to twenty-five years from the date of the event to be declared guilty of the offense by the sentient nexus pentarchy prime. Serious physical or spiritual harm has a statute of limitation of five years after the offense for a declaration of grave opinion determination for the offense. The exception is when a child is involved. The child has five years after being declared an adult by age or by pent-degree leader caretaker opinion when another has committed a serious physical or spiritual harm while the entity was a child.

Case Example: Uncontrolled Vehicle Use

Case Example:

Uncontrolled usage of a vehicle by an entity resulting in grave harm or in extinguishing another member in society.

Resolution:

The healing steps are:

1. Hold vehicle from entity.
2. Contain entity in camps.
3. Educate entity in the proper use of vehicle.
4. Impose a probation period for vehicle use.
5. Return the vehicle to the entity.

There ought to be a high degree of certainty that the harmful acts will not be repeated. Repeat violations by the entity will result in a five-fold duration increase in privilege removal for the entity. When it pertains to harmful acts, be clear regarding the seriousness of the events and the importance that serious containment actions are needed. Accidents are rarely "accidents" but due to the lack of preparations or blatant recklessness. Hence, prevention is the key to successful operation. Reckless operators will have their privileges suspended or revoked.

Case Consideration: Sizing Rape

The category of rape is historically considered to be one of grave endangerment to an adult entity. There is a tendency to overrate this violation especially when there is no convincing discoveries clearly identifying the event as such. Condemning provides no healing process to take place. Should there be misunderstanding of an entity's intent, then a decree will be issued that states the clear perspective of the entity who felt violated and that the entity who was perceived to be committing the harmful act to avoid proximity of the entity who felt violated. The proximity terms will be specific. Any violation of these terms will result in declaring the original event as a serious violation. The actions to be taken for serious violations are described elsewhere.

Case Consideration: Sizing Statutory Rape

A variance of five years separating the ages of two entities will be used to determine statutory rape as historically defined when an age is used for specifying automatic adulthood and the child did not consent to romantic encounters or was coerced. The category of statutory rape is historically considered to be one of grave endangerment to a minor. There is a tendency to overrate this violation especially when consenting entities are involved. Condemning provides no healing process to take place. The changes described above will aid in the healing process of all.

Statute of Limitations

Statutes of time limitation are needed in a variety of areas to include grave harmful events in order to measure performances of our executive and duty caretakers. No delays beyond the time limits will be accepted for general prime pool participation by any entity showing interest in discovery activities.

The Way to Uncover the Truth

The need to get out of the condemning business is great. By not condemning, a greater chance for uncovering the truth is very possible. Make it so and be surprise when it happens when you least expect it.

Nexus Prime Rapid Response Team

Nexus Prime Rapid Response Instrument Charter

The nexus prime rapid response instrument is chartered with peacekeeping duties to include apprehending and detaining entities that commit grave harmful acts. These duties will continue even in times of nexus pentarchy prime impasses when there is a suspension of further prime directive creation events. Sufficient resources will not be withheld.

Nexus prime rapid response teams comprised of five rapid deployment team members are formed to respond when on entity is committing grave harmful acts or are imminent. More teams are involved when there are more than one offending entity present.

Grave Harmful Truth Investigation Discoveries

Information discoveries learn as a result of truth investigator caretaking duties will only be revealed to the public or agencies when there are persuasive discovery findings in grave harmful acts. In certain situation, the dissemination of information may have to be withheld in protecting all entities involved. This is of prime importance! For example in the area of murder, which is the extinguishing of an entity, has been committed and there is a high degree of certainty that grave harmful acts will be committed but can be wisely prevented.

When discoveries do not pertain to grave harmful acts, the discoveries are confidential and the information cannot be disseminated beyond rapid response teams and the auspices of nexus prime. Findings will require to be re-discovered in matters involving non-harmful issue resolving requests, which may result in prime directives or opinions.

Nexus Officer Duty Caretakers

This is a classification of caretakers selected by the Auspices of the Sentient Nexus Pentarchy Prime in performing duties as members of the Rapid Deployment Teams in ensuring that the set of Universal Tenets and Axioms are not being violated by members anywhere.

Nexus Officer Duty Caretakers Removal

Rapid-response nexus executive duty caretakers can be removed with three of the five nexus pentarchy prime leader caretakers. The same as applies to all other degree prime designation of Officer Duty Caretakers.

Rapid Response Teams

A handful, five or fewer, of securing-the-peace personnel will intervene when one entity is killed. In this case, an automatic response team is made without approval of one or more of sentient nexus pentarchy prime leader caretakers. Escalation is warranted when killings of more than one entity exist. The response will be more paramilitary-like force sufficient enough to reduce the killings to zero. This situation ought to be rare. Also, periodic review of members of the response team is needed to ensure the best and wisest members are recruited and retained.

The most that a rapid response team officer caretaker can hold an entity is five days. Only a rapid response executive officer caretaker or auspices securing-the-peace caretaker of the sentient nexus pentarchy prime can hold one longer. A rapid response team caretaker (non-executive officer) can hold an entity for one day.

Alert Provisions

Alert provisions for missing members will be defined after twenty-five days since last contacted by the concerning party or when foul play is determined to happen by rapid response teams.

Producing and Implementing Containment Decrees

A decision made by executive officer caretakers delegated by leader caretakers can have up to twenty-five containment days given to members who fail to comply with issue review resolutions. Only the auspices of the sentient nexus leader caretakers will have the final determination pertaining to matters regarding entities that extinguish other entities. They may request a standing review board be formed to gather information and recommendations. Immediate containment orders are issued to those considered highly probable suspects, based on reliable eyewitnesses, and evidence produced by rapid response teams. Without formal investigation findings, orders up to five containment days can be made by rapid response team executive duty caretakers for the safety of all. Suspect officer duty caretakers will automatically be assigned to suspects, with liaison duties to handle all reasonable suspects' personal matters. They are different from suspect advocate officer caretakers, who review and challenge the charges made on the suspect's behalf. When a containment sentencing outcome is made, the only reason for discharge is when new information overwhelmingly clears a suspect or after a minimum of twenty-five years and there is a very high degree of certainty that no

further harm will be done by the entity once
released into society. The twenty-five year limit
is given to entities when the gravity of the
harmful events was of the highest of grievous acts.
In the event that a second sentencing is made for
capital offenses, life containment is automatic
without release. A high degree of certainty from
suspects committing further harm would then have
been shown.

Confinement and Release

A nexus pentarchy prime rapid response team
executive caretaker can hold a dangerous entity
until final investigation findings or set free due
to convincing evidence to the contrary.

Duty Peace Caretakers

Honorable and inspiring are the duty peace
caretakers.

Containment Environments

Historical Containment Views

Historically, court-ordered jail terms are nothing more than "time outs" for members of society. Jails ought to be for the security of communities and not to house members because of social issues that are not being adequately addressed. Think about this for a moment.

Dungeons Obsolete

The game of dungeons will no longer be played.

Non-Growth Industry

Prisons will no longer be promoted as an industry. Historical trends will not be used to build more prisons. A service will be provided by nexus prime to confine entities that are shown to exhibit grave harm to other non-threatening entities of the prime. When the numbers become large, urgent discovery activities are performed to determine hidden causes that can be rectified and return prime to favorable conditions. Action plans based on these findings will be implemented.

Minimal Containment Numbers

The incarcerating of large numbers of entities is not acceptable. Only the auspices of the nexus prime will make that decision in times of grave emergencies. We are choosing to promote the health and vitality of all members of the nexus prime.

F. Dot

Containment Duration

Five years minimum confinement is required due to an accidental negligence that resulted in a death. An accidental negligence is when the accident has a high degree of certainty that the accident could have been avoided by entities in a pool of similar vocation using the Rule of Five to make that test.

Twenty-five years minimum confinement required due to purposeful acts leading to death. A purposeful act is when there is a certain degree of time and planning in committing the grave harmful acts.

In all confinement cases when an entity is extinguish by the entity in confinement and after serving a minimal duration, a very high degree of certainty must still exist that the entity will not repeat the harmful act again before the entity can be released from confinement.

Non-Capital Offense Duration

Containment for non-life extinguishing offenses will never be greater than the average duration in murder containment opinions. The primary concern must remain to separate violent entities from the more peaceful ones.

Violators Housed

Violators who are confined for offenses will be housed or camped with others of similar offenses. No mixing of violent and non-violent offenders is permitted.

Degrees of Confinement

More secure confinements are for those members who have performed acts of grave violence. There will be degrees of confinement based on the severity of the events and ongoing interactions with other members within confinement facilities.

Minimum Containment Facilities

Non-violent violators will not be housed in such maximum containment facilities. They will be housed in minimum containment facilities or camps. Duty caretakers carrying no firearms or weapons of any kind will guard non-violent facilities. These facilities will be self-directing containment camps whereby the tenants will learn by managing their own care.

Detainment Camps

Detainment camps are defined as limited access to confined entities whereby focused education and training avenues are provided to enable the return of entities to umbrella primes. While in these camps, entities must also cooperate with others in the camp for basic needs. Abusers of privileges will result in more restricting confinement with other similar abusers. Self-directing training is needed to gradually return to general detainment pools.

Privilege Scale

Those entities in confinement will have reduced privileges. The degree of reduced privileges depends on the degree of severity in the entities' behaviors and actions.

Protected Separations

High security confinement facilities are to be used for very violent offenders. Confinement camps of varying degrees of security will be used for other offenders. No mixing of non-violent offenders with violent ones is allowed.

It's a Certainty

Containment of entities who commit grave harmful acts at other entities is generally viewed to be a certainty. A very high degree of certainty is needed and required to permit the offending entities to return to free primes once again. Much time is needed for such a consideration. Be patient.

Victims Have Input Rights to Remedy Resolution

When an entity is contained for offenses, there will be no caged lock-up unless violent offenses have been made and the victim who experienced the offense has agreed. Exception is when the victim is dead and the one closest to the victim will take her place in making that determination and when determination that violent tendencies have greatly subsided. Entities will manage their own care while in containment with sufficient resources for survival needs. No torture or execution of anyone in captivity will be allowed, ever!

When Confinement Term Limits Are Not Given

There will never be an order specifying duration for grave harmful committing entities. No violent person is allowed to be set free because no "timed" orders will be given, even if it means for life!

The person will be set free when there is a high degree of trust and certainty that that person will not do similar acts of violence again and after spending a pre-defined universally applied minimum confinement duration.

Maximum Containment Facilities

When it comes to violent or grave violations to another entity or entities, containment is immediate with no end date. A minimum duration must be met which will equal the longest duration for non-serious or the least violent violations, whichever is greater. Any release after the minimum time will be granted when an extremely high certainty is realized whereby no serious and violent violations will ever occur again. The containment will be in maximum security and restricted facilities that confine only tenants that have committed similar grave violations. Duty caretakers of these facilities are permitted to protect themselves.

The Caretaking of Containment Facilities

There are those duty caretakers who will say that they were not involved with criminal acts that may occur in containment facilities. For auspices executive officer duty caretakers however, if many such acts did in fact occur on their watch, then their title of auspices executive officer duty caretaker will to be stripped from them. The aim is to have the best auspices executive officer duty caretakers in charge.

F. Dot

No Executions on My Watch

No executions will occur on my watch. If you permit that to occur on your watch, your sentient awareness has been greatly diminished.

Escape Remedy

The mere fact that a violent entity is placed in containment ought to make the umbrella primes secure. The containment is to be in a maximum-security facility. Auspices executive officer duty caretakers whose watches permit escape of those in maximum containment will be scrutinized and a determination made whether to have them replaced immediately. The duty caretakers being closest to the elements ought to be aware of such situations in advance. No violence will be done to those in containment is the primary rule when non-violent behavior is present by any entity. Forcible apprehension is permitted for those who continue violence to any entity around them.

Violent Issues Scope

Decisive Actions

Historically, there was a notion that the law will punish those who commit unspeakable crimes like murder. In fact, laws must first be passed that define harmful acts as crimes before these same acts can even be considered crimes. In the mean time, the killings continue because of delays in ensuring supposedly a person's rights. What is better is to have leader caretakers take decisive actions to contain those who have the highest probability of committing a serious offense based on available evidence. After a full inquiry and deliberation, the entity in confinement will be released or kept in confinement for the safety of all when that is the conclusion or opinion.

Grave Harm

It is important to contain entities whose purpose is to cause grave harm to others.

Response for Member Killers

Historically, the notion that someone who kills another is set free after a not-guilty verdict is simply not valid. The sentient nexus pentarchy prime leader caretakers are the only ones who have the ultimate responsibility to review containment of dangerous persons after new evidence is forthcoming.

The need to isolate threatening entities is great.

Condemning is going Out of Business

We will be out of the condemning business soon if not already. The business of condemning leads to our own destruction. Rapid deployment teams will have been required to process through rigorous selection process and training to become our supreme peace protection restoring caretakers. Characteristic traits are honesty, integrity, ethics, and wisdom in determining sufficient force solutions. Weapons of greater than required mass destruction will not be used. Executive peace caretaker of the rapid peace restoring team can determine low yield firepower defensive weapons usage. Non firepower and non-lethal weapons usage can be left to a member of rapid deployment team. In all cases where grave harmful events do occur, leader caretaker reviews are required. Valid use of non-lethal force is reviewed with the assistance of the pent-degree ascension prime.

Accountability for All Killings and Suspicious Deaths

All killings or suspicious deaths must be looked into. This is the ultimate responsibility of the sentient nexus pentarchy prime leader caretakers and their instruments. They may appoint investigators to look into the matter. However, the final determination responsibility still rests with them. Of course, it is natural to assume that these five nexus leader caretakers would be wise in selecting necessary auspices consultancies to assist with timely opinions. Consider stepping forward when asked to.

Murder Investigations

Investigations of murders are open-ended. However, twenty-five years will be given as active status by the sentient nexus pentarchy prime. After twenty-five years, private concerns may take up the investigation and have access to all information collected to date and that will be collected by truth investigation duty caretakers and auspices consultancies in the future.

Truth Discoveries

For serious harmful events, every entity must tell the truth during prime directing inquiry sessions. Those that were discovered to not have given true testimonies with more than a reasonable certainty will be confined in multiples of five days up to a maximum of 125 days based on severity of the false statements and resulting outcomes.

On the Side of Caution

Nexus leader caretakers can determine that an entity or entities can be confined as part of suspicious entity death investigation exhaustive findings to date, even when there is not persuasive evidence at the time. However, without very convincing evidence, the confinement is for a maximum of five years. Should more convincing evidence be forthcoming and are within its guidelines, then the conclusive confinement rules prevail. Should more persuasive evidence indicate that a member is innocent, release is immediate after discovery.

Official Endangerment

Officials whose orders result in grave harm to an entity or entities when an entity or entities are themselves not committing grave harm to others or is imminent, are to be considered dangerous for purposes of containment. Containment will continue until a high degree of certainty is achieved that a repeat of grave decisions and actions that could follow will not be made.

Assassination Response

When a leader caretaker is assassinated, everything within the prime stops that does not involve vital prime services while the prime is scoured for information and remedies! No further decisions are made until the investigation is complete.

Prime Privileged Information

A "hold" status on an entity is made when the entity has done a gravest act requiring containment. Information regarding the entity is privileged during this time to investigative discovery activity caretakers until significant conclusive findings are forthcoming.

Defender Duty Caretakers Assignments

Defender duty caretakers will aid in the investigation and advocacy of a defendant who has been sent to high security confinement.

On the Side of Safety

Consider being on the side of safety when an entity is determine to have a very high probability of being the one who committed a grave offense. Have the entity in confinement for the safety of all parties involved to include the entity in confinement.

Extinguish Issues Scope

Extinguish

The deliberate extinguishing of entities in corporeal form is the premier focus of resources and time by the sentient nexus pentarchy prime. The nexus prime can rely on all degree primes assistance in their investigations and remedies.

Measured Responses

Measured responses may be needed to contain or extinguish violent actions. No excessive actions are permitted.

Sufficient Force Application

Those who knowingly or purposefully participate in the decision and/or execution of grave harmful acts in the guise of dealing with other entities' grave harmful acts will be viewed as committing similar acts. The exception is when performed while protecting oneself or selves. Only rapid response teams are given the latitude to provide measured responses when needed.

Percolate to the Top

Unless an entity departs by natural means, the gravity of the departure will percolate up to the top of the ascension primes and be detected by the nexus prime for investigation and remedy.

Non-Natural Departure

Only when extinguishing of corporeal existence is by non-natural causes will the nexus prime be involved. Questionable causes that may or may not be by natural causes will be investigated first by the pent-degree ascension prime. Acceleration to nexus prime is made immediately when a reasonable assertion is made regarding non-natural causes. Nexus prime have unlimited access to review information regarding all such happenings and conclusions. Periodically, nexus prime will choose selected cases for review.

Progress Reports

Provision for Confinement in Error

Since there is always a chance that an entity may be confined in error, once a new review followed by a new hearing has been conducted because significant new information and validations are uncovered, release is immediate, in less than twenty-five hours.

Dangerous Environments and Remedies

Robe of Violence Advocacy

Our historical criminal justice system will be dismantled due to its premise that members of society must be condemned so that its framework can exist. Do not be fooled in its view that justice is served when entities are condemned. This framework cannot hide behind its "robe of violence advocacy".

Stop Property Holdings Form of Terrorism

Stop terrorism in all its forms. In nation-state frameworks, citizens are properties and owned by the nation-state that declares them. When sentient entities are hunted down like criminals because of artificial legal status of being a non-citizen and that is the only reason for the hunt, then that act of apprehension is terrorism. Where is the humanity in this, this property-holdings premise by antiquated feudal lords?

Retiring Non-Issue Incarcerations

It is abominable to incarcerate entities whose only crime is the passion to be free to associate with any group and to go anywhere in the pool's reach. When no harm is being done to other entities or to environments, these behaviors are to be unrestricted when the impact is minimal. Let's retire these non-issue incarcerations.

In the Same Environment

Historically, benefits for soldiers in campaigns were provided regardless if severe harm was experienced or not. This was not so for members with medical problems. During those times, benefits must be determined first based on health diagnosis before a graduated degree of assistance is provided. In Pentarchy Prime framework when entities are in the same environment, generally, benefits will be covered as well.

Sufficient Force Doctrine

Significantly more force than what can be done with sufficient minimal force that is sanctioned by historical nation-state is never acceptable. Gradual reduction in the use of force will be one of many purposes of primes. This is possible because those who are closest to the serious issues are more effective in resolving the issue. Choose not to turn back the historical clock in the harsh and overkill application in the use of excessive force.

Reduced to Rounding up Violent Entities

Historically, the reason for nation-state wars is because citizens are not allowed to leave! When entities are allowed to leave hostile environments, the actions are reduced to rounding up violent entities using rapid response teams. It will then be learned that far fewer entities are in fact violent by nature.

Die-Hard Spies

Spies that infiltrate primes with the objective of disrupting and dismantling the foundation will be exposed and identified within the prime framework to all prime members. A severe banishment is declared with the added directive that no further issue-resolution requests can be reviewed involving spies that violate applicable prime directives. The time period of banishment will be in multiples of five years up to twenty-five years, depending on severity. This information will be provided to all ascension primes to include the nexus prime. These degree primes will make appropriate prime directives for themselves.

Ecological Impact Activities

The harmful ecological impact activities produced by historical military framework do jeopardize national security. If allowed to continue, eventually, there will be no one else to argue on its use. Is this wise? These activities may have won the wars but loose the peace and nature's subsistence ways for the viable environment. Nature will make corrections based on usage. Nature reacts in time when it is raped.

Urgent Pursuits

An urgent pursuit of pentarchy primes, when it arise, is the dismantling of terrorist activities.

Hostilities Relocation

During the transitional period to pentarchy primes, entities joining the primes from hostile nation-states will be relocated far from the boundaries of these hostile nation-states. This safety measure is provided so long as the entities did not commit grave harmful acts anywhere that were not in self-defense. A vast barrier will have to be traveled for nation-states to impose forced repatriations. Any actions by these feudal nation-states will demonstrate their true terrorist persona.

Rapid Shut Down

If any agency is found to conduct terrorist activities, it will be shut down. It does not matter that a small part of the agency is conducting these activities or not. When discovered that these activities did in fact take place, the opinion will be that there is an element that is a fabric of the agency that is fundamentally amiss. If the agency is still needed as an instrument of Pentarchy Prime then it will be rebuilt from foundation zero. Executive officer caretakers will have to reapply. Once selected, then the general duty caretakers will be reassigned when it is warranted.

A Call to all Sentients

We will work towards breaking up all terrorist-producing organizations anywhere in the known world and beyond whose charters promote violent actions directed at other sentient entities as defined by prime tenets and directives.

Prime Member Impersonators

Offer no assistance and walk away from easy assistance and resources from convert prime member impersonators. Follow prime umbrella directives only. The built-in prime activities will expose these impersonators. With prime membership and related activities, the numbers are against impersonators from dismantling primes.

Contributing Actors

When accidents or grave events do take place, investigations are performed as to the cause. When it is found that caretakers, those holding positions that are chartered with preventive activities, were contributing actors in these events, then they are banned from their positions for specified periods of time. The duration is based on the severity of the neglect.

Urgent Happenings

When communications are cut off and information that is being spread cannot be confirmed, state it so to all who requests it and caution them not to take it as fact for the time being until further inquiry discoveries can be made. Use procedures regarding separation from umbrella primes during emergencies. Prime directives that are produced but may be in conflict with the greater umbrella prime will not be admonished because of separation. However, all known prime directives and tenets will be recognized and carried out. Exception is in times of grave emergencies.

Natural Boundaries Instrument Charter

Identify and post natural boundaries subject to nature's laws. Interactions by prime members are at their own risks. Exclusions are when hazards produced by prime members within twenty-five years. Hazards produced by prime members are to be removed by the same members. Violators will be subject to stiff penalties and removal of related privileges when there is failure to comply.

Periodic Safe Passage Convoys

Frequent unannounced passage convoys will travel the domains in order to provide entities the opportunity to join the convoy. These convoys are opportunities to rescue oppressed entities or entities with self-directing pursuits. The awareness that we are all part of a greater pool is ever present.

Transitional Governance Reach

Nation-State Transformation

One by one, when the historical nation-state frameworks are replaced with umbrella primes, all agreements made to other external nation-states will be terminated and outstanding issues referred to the corresponding umbrella primes having span proximity to the frameworks. Rules and guidelines described elsewhere apply in these situations.

The Folding of Nation-States

One by one, nation-states will be declared obsolete and all prior contracts or treaties created when the nation-states were operational will be null and void. The complete suite of prime directives will be in effect everywhere.

Terrorist Officials Removal

Members holding ancient legislative official or representative positions who have passed laws of terror as defined by pentarchy primes will be expeditiously removed and replaced with others who are selected by primes to hold these transitional office-holding positions during the transitional period.

Pentarchy Prime "Elected Officials"

Primes are charter with issuing prime directives when needed. Other non-leader caretakers are required to take effective actions when asked to by leader caretakers that span their domains. Those who fail to perform their duties, as decree, will be subject to removal from their positions. This includes those who are "elected" by mass elections in historical governing systems. All prime directives covering "elected officials" are to be published for all to see within the umbrella prime.

Freedom of Movement

Terrorism exists when a nation-state prohibits free movements of sentients when the only "crimes" that were acted on were to cross artificial-borders (man-made ones). When there are no other detainment orders in effect, they must be allowed to freely pass without restrictions. The only restrictions are those established by pentarchy primes. The nation-state holds no ownership of sentients. Pentarchy primes will pursue every effort possible in making this so.

Guilty by Association

The state that requires its citizens to do the police work based on its punitive laws regarding unlawful statutes in the area of providing humane behaviors and treatments toward "enemies (criminals) of the state" who commit "criminal" acts is shunning its responsibilities in these matters. No law ought to exist that make it a crime for any entity who helps in humane ways and not be aware of past, present, or future grave harmful acts. If we truly are to have a caring world, then no caring behavior will be prohibited.

Interim State Monopolies

Level the playing field by insisting on nation-state's monopolies for both prosecutions and defenses. Having one without the other reinforces the framework that lopsided abuses are ever present.

Restitution

Restitution, monetary or other forms, for events caused prior to pentarchy prime ascension will not be reviewed for remedies. After pentarchy prime arrival, restitution will have no meaning. It is very unlikely that any "awards" will be granted if basic needs are being supported. The focus is on uncovering root causes for failure to optimally provide caretaking activities that benefit all. In this way, corrective-action decrees can be taken and be ever present. In summary, there will be assistance not compensation, there will be assistance not restitution.

The Leashing of Politicians

Historical politicians have the propensity to be political. This is due to their training and limited view. That's all they know how to do. Our interest is to ensure that all our decisions are carried out and to remove anyone whom fails to comply. The politicians that are in violation will lose all privileges bestowed by the prime for significant periods of time up to twenty-five years.

Interim Courts

Historical courts can exist in the interim when no harmful acts are involved. Otherwise, leader caretakers have ownership and responsibility of decision/opinion outcome.

Declarations of Transfers

When primes supersedes the decision making of nation governing bodies, declarations made by these pre-prime governing agency bodies will be declared at the end of their life cycle. The historical agencies will be either shut down or transformed into prime agencies with new principles of conduct and objectives.

The End to War Machines

War machines will be dismantled. Rapid deployment teams will be created with its primary charter of diminishing and extinguishing entities' or groups of entities' violent activities no matter where these activities may be found. The nexus pentarchy prime is supremely responsible for its charter and oversight with command centers located throughout all umbrella primes.

Cartels

All historical non-violent entity-limiting government sponsored elite cartels are to be dismantled.

Time and Energy Well Spent

Do not expend much time and energy with historical governmental agencies in trying to persuade them to do the right thing. Instead, the focus ought to be on persuading and at times removing "official" non-prime caretakers whom no longer are capable of making wise decisions on behalf of all.

Heighten Terrorist State

During the transitional period, be mindful of renegade nation-states that violate prime directives. This may be an indication of a heightened terrorist state.

Warning/Advisory during Transition

When possible, it is unwise to make any agreements with a non-pentarchy prime member until such time that no other non-caretaker system exists or has collapsed. When that happens, agreements are based on pentarchy prime rules and guidelines.

We will perform no bartering with those pentarchy prime members caught in the containment snare of the non-caretaker system. The premise that no entity is a form of property prevails in this case. Activities and events over time will result in their release. However, we will provide timely escape assistance to all members in grave circumstances.

One Sided View of Prisoners of War

During the transitional period, if a nation-state uses the military to contain the populace of any other nation-state, then the opposing populous are soldiers of their campaign (issue). If captured by this nation-state's military, they are to be considered prisoners of war (POW). When "orders" are given for military action by this nation-state, their argument that only their soldiers can have POW distinction is a terrorist view. The reasoning is that the military is chartered for war. War results in prisoners of war in all cases.

In pentarchy primes, there will be no need to go to war. Release of "prisoners" will have no meaning.

The whole concept of POW will become irrelevant everywhere. Containment for those who have the propensity to commit grave harmful acts is a prime directive.

Non-Pentarchy Prime Officeholder

One's measure of compliance by officeholder in non-pentarchy prime frameworks is based on whether prime directives are being implemented. If not, no further decision or discussion with that officeholder will be made until prior decision is carried out. The officeholder will be removed from her position. Removal activities will commence at the earliest possible time for serious non-compliant activities.

Focus on Leaders

Focus on senior official actors who are self-appointed or forced imposed surrogates that interfere with our leader caretakers. Remove anyone from position of authority in historical belief systems when she fails to carry out our prime decisions. Do not be distracted with institutions with their methods and ways. They exist at the pleasure of our leader caretakers. Those who resist will have an entry made in their Pentarchy Prime public record stating that the entity or entities will be prohibited from holding compatible caretaker positions for twenty-five years commencing on the day that the member is removed from position. This is to be viewed as a very serious offense.

Interim Entry Points

Do not be concern initially with commercial and cultural exchanges with the known world. Work with your neighbors first. The affect will be like rainwater that eventually goes into creeks, then streams, then rivers, then lakes, and then oceans. Insist that nation-state laws be just and not violate basic prime tenets. There will be points into shared pools of primes. Eventually, only primes exist, which are something quite wonderful to strive for.

Implementation Plan for World Mobility

The implementation plan for gradual world mobility is first to have neighboring nation-states have freedom to cross their borders within five months of declaration with gradual entire world mobility completed in five years.

Transitional Commerce Center Embassies

Transitional Commerce Center Embassies (TCCE) will replace in the interim separate prime and non-prime centers for any issue involving both frameworks regarding commerce. The stewards will be comprised of five members from prime and five members from non-prime members. For the possible gradual implementation of resolution, three votes from the non-prime pools and three votes from prime pools are needed. For immediate implementation of resolution, four or more votes from each pool are needed.

Guests or Visitors

While non-prime members are within prime domains, prime directives regarding guests or visitors must be observed and vice versus. In order for TCCEs to exist, execution of detainees anywhere is strictly prohibited. When discoveries of executions are found, TCCEs' are temporarily closed until corrective actions are forthcoming and verifiable. Investigators will have unrestricted access to any confinement facilities for verification regarding any reported abuse discovered anywhere.

Society Member Sentencing Compliance

While in transition to prime framework, when a member of society fulfills conditions of sentencing, then no restrictions from having a job can be imposed. The only criteria for employment will be on job performances and other ancillary activities. This is reflective of pentarchy prime directives.

No Persuasion Needed

Until pentarchy prime immersion, the elitists are a very small part of the world's population. Hence, there is no need to persuade them to join our foundation primes. By selecting officials who implement prime directives, their elitist ranks will dwindle and fall like an avalanche.

Reach of "Political" Review

To conserve time, resources, and the prevention of errors, focus on historical political spectrum domains whereby the Rule of Five prevails as it pertains to interactions with pentarchy prime and resulting outcomes.

Oath of Understanding

All who passes through primes must commit themselves to prime foundation governance or be treated as temporary guests with very limited access and privileges. Their oath of understanding must be clear to them or their pass-through must be speedy. In the latter case when pass-through is not speedy, then they will be escorted through the prime quickly.

Transitional Governance Instruments

To Whom the Courts Serve

During the transitional period, historical courts serve at the pleasure of the prime caretakers. This is strongly advised. When prime instruments are effectively in place, these courts will be given expiration dates. The time is near.

Interim Elected Officials

As part of the transition towards primes exclusively, officials selected to fill elected offices are on probation once elected. Failure to promote prime directives will lead to removal from office at the earliest possible time, e.g., the next election or preferably a recall. More than one recall or election may be needed as pentarchy prime framework gains universal appeal.

Universal Care Support Amount

During the transition period, what the tax code states as the amount for dependent deduction, then that is the universal child-care support amount needed to raise a child based on these enacted "laws". In this way, no child will have a higher "value" than another. This amount will be used in all "child support payment" amount determinations. Eventually, children will no longer be property of anyone or man-made artifact.

Public Relations

No questions by non-member entities will be answered freely. Consultation with leader caretakers whose umbrella pentarchy prime encompasses the effective reach in non-prime domains will be made for the review and any subsequent response that may be needed.

Interim "Free" Elections

While there are "free" elections for elected duty officials, the selection of officials that carry out prime directives will be promoted. Failure to comply by any elected official will result in dismissal activities. The selection of the lessor of two evils will not be considered. When no viable candidate is available, write-ins of the chosen candidate will be promoted.

Obsolete N-Tier Courts

After transitions, there will be no n-tier justice systems as they pertain to quality and uniformity of the entire process. These systems based on nation-state land holdings to include sentients will have no meaning.

Interim Court Resolutions

During the transitional era towards total pentarchy prime framework, new court resolution must specify duration for prohibition on privileges. For prior resolutions, an automatic twenty-five year cap will be made in all cases not involving grave harmful acts.

Interim Official Review and Selection

During the transformational era towards pentarchy prime foundation, umbrella primes are chartered in producing directives regarding who in the current political spectrum must resign or face future long-term privilege limiting directives. In addition, identify all those in the current political spectrum who have consistently and dutifully carried out prime directives. Also a candidate rating system will be architect and implemented based on prime perspectives and acceptable scores. There can be multiple candidates selected and promoted by umbrella primes for the same official position. The rating will aid prime members as to the proper voter selection.

Peaceful Strategy

By following a strategy of peaceful primes, we will expose the framework's violent "trigger-points" of nation-states. One by one, these points will be erased. In time, these artifact frameworks will collapse.

Interim Attorneys

During the transitional period, all "criminal" attorneys will be transferred to serving the public interest. Truth discovery pursuits will replace an adversarial system of posturing. No one is to be condemned. Wise courses of action will be promoted instead. Do not be fooled, effective remedies will be issued.

Multiparty Decline

Vying for territorial (land) use exclusivity by the two-party political system has no meaning in primes. Wise leader caretakers understand the needs and issues of umbrella primes. Caretaking is taken seriously. Checks and balances are in place to ensure that this is so.

Test the Limits

We will test the limits of perceived "democratic systems" and then some until these elitist systems implode. Do not be fooled on the true nature of democratic systems. They are based on exclusion. Pentarchy primes will then become universal.

One by One

One by one during the transitional period, laws that violate prime directives will be nullified. Courts then cannot pass rulings based on laws that no longer exist.

A Monopoly in Both Arenas

If the judicial system of an historical framework has a monopoly on prosecutions, then it will also be chartered to have a monopoly on the defense. In its historical existence, the system is not just. By having a dual system with prosecution and defense given monies in equal amounts by the artifact institution, both sides are served. Sharing of common services such as scientific analysis or access to any information permitted by either would be wise and cost-effective. Nation-state "legal institutions" will not have a monopoly in providing only prosecution services.

In addition, a historical "grand" jury will be comprised of skilled truth investigators when needed. Conscripts are not to be used. The premise is that it will be primarily chartered to uncover the truth so as to assist in a humane response to serious offenses. Therefore, those skilled in truth discoveries need apply. No condemning is permitted.

Bail Baggage

Bail concept baggage is a carryover of property rights and is no longer valid in a pentarchy prime framework. Do not be fooled. No entity can hide for long. Therefore, bail is of little aid. Failure to appear will lead to more severe consequences. If entity actions pertain to grave harmful events towards other entities, then containment is immediate. No release is possible unless investigative discoveries proved otherwise. This is described elsewhere.

Realm of Business

The realm of business is adequately served in the interim by the judicial system as historically constructed. Note that this belief system is meant to include the judicial, legislative, and executive branches. This belief system is an interim one that will evolve into a more streamlined one.

Nation-State Defense Monopoly

Let it be emphasized that if a nation-state is going to have a monopoly in prosecuting a member of a society, then the state will also have a monopoly in providing the defense with access to all information collected by the prosecution team, and vice versa.

Fairness for State Monopolies

For balance to exist should we choose to continue in the interim with the historical judicial belief system, the same amount of resources should be allocated to the defense of those that are being charged. It should not be considered unreasonable for a state institution to provide for such services, especially when it holds a monopoly in areas of prosecutions, since members of society cannot initiate prosecution proceedings themselves. We need truth investigation caretakers and not executioners.

Information Freely Recorded

There historically exists the legal notion that "evidential proofs" must be presented to reveal any truths. For the sake of argument, let us say yes. However, information should be freely recorded without censorship of opinions and ideas. They may be admissible. The information can be tagged accordingly. The passage of time and questioning of those who testify will validate the accuracy of their testimonies.

Time Limits on Business Laws

There will be an expiration date for all historical business laws passed even when other laws are built on top of them. If the validity of such laws still exists, the laws must be passed again.

The reasoning is that artificial (man-made) laws are to be viewed as not being cast in stone. The set of all laws ebb and flow just like the history of sentients. It is only when rigidity for ancient laws exists that the framework snaps and implodes.

Re-passage of Laws

Historical laws over twenty-five years old are either re-passed as current laws or are made void by default on the twenty-fifth anniversary since the passage of the respective law. Within five years prior to the expiration of a particular law, a law can be re-passed. The initial enforcement of this rule will permit all laws falling outside the twenty-five-year limit an extra five years to have the laws reviewed for possible re-passage. They can be determined to be re-passed on a case by case basis or when it makes more sense to group related laws together and re-pass them as one package to preserve cohesion.

Non-Harmful Dispute Resolution

A proposal that each entity or group in a dispute be allowed to pick, say, two members from the community to form a review and resolution panel, with a tie-breaker coming from the auspices of the jurist pool. It is the jurist pool that will be composed of experts or professionals trained to handle matters requiring resolution. Both sides will select this tie-breaker jurist. It is this system that will return power back to the members of society.

Interim Issue Resolution Instrument

The judicial system as it pertains to non-grave harmful acts can be maintained for some time until established pentarchy prime instruments are in place. Judges can only jail entities up to twenty-five days. Twenty-five days out of jail must pass before a repeat can be made when the offense is still the original one. Only leader caretakers can extend a stay longer when violent offenses occur or when imminent killings exist. The aim is to secure the peace using all resources available. No use of lethal force will be permitted unless serious life extinguishing acts or serious bodily harmful acts are in progress.

F. Dot

Withdrawal Prime Directive

When prime directives are made to withdraw from selected non-prime organizations and operations in the most expeditious manner, do so without causing grave harm to yourself.

Universal Passports

An interim transformation directive is to have what historically is known as the World Body provide universally recognized passports to be used to gain unobstructed passage anywhere in the known universe. Denial can only be made for entities that have been found to commit grave harmful acts or the imminent findings that potential grave harmful acts could have been committed had the acts not been kept in check.

Indicators for Interim Corrections

During the transitional period, officials must comply with prime directives even when other current institutions file suit against them in the courts. The ruling will indicate where changes will need to be made in either the laws or the constitutional framework. The offending parts will be dismantled. Umbrella primes will provide assistance to personal matters when prime-selected officials are in confinement.

Prime Directives Shall Prevail

When there is a conflict of interest between official directives while an entity is an office holder in an historical framework and prime directives, then prime directives shall prevail. Office holders will need to resign when "orders" are given that require them to violate prime directives.

Transformational Plan

One by one, nation-states that transform into primes will quietly withdraw members, resources, and money exchanges before announcing exits from treaties not recognizing primes as the supreme issue-resolution-decision-making instruments. When the historical "great" land (war) lords threaten in the use of force to return primes back to nation-states (war lords), they will have demonstrated how "feudal" and unjust they truly are. Do not respond with military responses. These "just war lords" will find that their own feudal members will dismantle their own systems when they learn that violence is being done on non-violent members. Ruling over the masses will be shown to be unwieldy. We have safety in numbers.

Transitional Identification Documents

Historical nation-states issued "passport" identification documents to members of their respective limited-access "societies" and must be shown to any other nation-state that is visited. Should there be a need for identification tags used for speedy processing, the universal "world body" will issue universal entity speed instruments instead. No denial of entry is permitted unless containment of an entity is necessary because of grave harmful acts committed to others.

Time-Delayed Prime Directives

Prime decisions are to be made even when they cannot be carried out in the early phase of prime creation. Prime decisions will be recorded and archived for future implementation. Time is on our side. In time, all prime directives will be carried out. It is folly to think otherwise. The apparent delay will quite likely be due to the recognition that grave harmful acts can be avoided or minimized. During the transitional period, the only reason when prime directives cannot be carried out is when they violate basic tenets or conflict with more ascension prime directives that are discovered later.

The Framework of Caretaking

No Provisions for a Waiting Period

History shows that there was a notion that laws protect members of nation-states from grave harmful acts. However, if laws do not exist for specific categories of grave harmful acts, no laws have been violated and hence, it is viewed as when no grave harmful acts have been committed. It this situation, how can society be really protected and secure? This is then the Archilles' heel in this type of law-based framework. The time lags for corrective responses cause more harmful acts to be experienced. *Prime framework waits for no provisions* when leader caretakers are chartered with unobstructed responsibility for wise resolution. Adjustments are immediate when determined to be on the side of caution when harmful acts are present or imminent.

At-Large Checks and Balances

The elite are just that. There are not many of them. For vast majority of members in society to grant vast powers to a few is alarming! Do select your leader caretakers wisely and allow them to make wise decisions. Our numbers are very large. With primes, there are checks and balances with the method of de-selecting leader caretakers when there is a history of unwise decision-making. Why minimize your importance and involvement? Be counted!

Uncovering the Truths Framework

The criminal courts as historically defined will transform from a defense plea of "guilty/not guilty" to one of uncovering the truths. Except for

grave offenses when insufficient evidences exist,
the charges, if declared, will be dropped and
entity or entities are to be released. Twenty-five
day confinement is the limit in these situations of
truth discoveries with a moderate certainty. Only
supreme auspices for the nexus leader caretakers
and the leader caretakers themselves can detain
entities for longer than twenty-five days for grave
harmful acts.

Decision Balancing Assured

With the historical judicial system, the vast
majority of decisions are reserved to a very small
number of members in society. With primes, the vast
majority of decisions are reserved to the vast
number of members in society through its umbrellas'
span-caretaking reach. Sizing the decisions
promotes every member's participation.

Good Samaritans Welcomed

Historically, Good Samaritans were no longer
welcomed because of restrictive criminal code
against assisting labeled criminals with even basic
survival needs. By having only a humanitarian
perspective ought not to be a crime. It will be
viewed as a grave harmful act when others do
offending acts while in their care, such as
possession of illegal weapons. Remove one's self
when discoveries of this kind exist and work with
auspices truth investigators.

Caretakers Needed

Historical judges are not caretakers. They are
instead, administrators. Sentient well being is too
important to be left solely to administrators.
Caretakers are needed instead. Caretakers that are

involved with the health and welfare of entities are best able to handle them. Caretakers are asked to apply.

Protected Shield

The protected shield factor goes up when primes freely produce their own prime directives. Autocratic land lords will have a most difficult time forcing their will on primes. Their castles and security motes will decay and return to Earth's domain. Their frameworks are short-lived.

Natural Environments Usage and Oversight

Hunting and fishing privileges will be allowed to interested entities. However, auspices for nature's promotion executive officer caretakers' rules and guidelines will be adhered to. Violations can lead to privileges being revoked for a specified period of time.

Sanctuaries

Refuge of various kinds is like an oasis for species that are protected. These refuges will include those identified for sentients as well. Survival for all forms of expressions is assured provided these expressions do not violate basic tenets.

Harvest Yields

When "fishing the oceans of the world" for food, the fine tuning methods for yielding the greatest catch to the extreme will not be promoted. The methods that promote sustainable and/or return to historical ocean life populations and gains will be used and refined instead. The framework of caretaking applies here as well.

Inclusive Perspectives

It is important not to exclude anyone. All who are no longer in confinement are to be included. All perspectives are needed to make very wise decisions for domain vitality.

Charter of Care!

Very valid reasonable attempts will be made by environmental resource extraction duty caretakers. The "Charter of Care" will be created that defines directives that will promote the environment to renew itself. Design and construction of sentient habitats and work sites will be such as to minimize adverse impacts on the environment.

A Noble Trait

It is a noble trait to save others from harm even when harm is possible for one's self. The spirit grows when a way is found.

Hoarding

Hoarding of resources and claims on them are not in the best interest of primes. Resources are for the benefit of all. No ownership is allowed. Leasing to resource extracting caretakers for the benefit of all is allowed.

Returned to Prime Pool

Failure to comply with prime directives can lead to the return of land and property stewardships back to prime pool.

Hope for the Innocent

With the prime directive of no execution of an entity in confinement, this provides unending hope to save innocent ones.

Nature Bounty

Provide some resources to those few passionate entities that are protecting or making inquiries on the environment that indicate preservation and nature bounty promotions. The return will be bountiful.

Equalizing Support

There will exist no property and/or values attributed to entities in any issue review and resolution proceedings. Only equalizing support assistance can be considered. For example, suppose that there is a monetary support value given for every child. Those caretakers who can afford will be required to provide this value. Those caretakers who cannot effectively support this value will provide a level of support based on their financial portfolio and are not forgiven for the difference in monetary support. The payment in full is required over time.

Unrestricted Access

All pentarchy prime leader caretakers in the immediate degree minus-one foundation primes within a particular umbrella prime are to be given unrestricted access as spectators to umbrella prime activities. The only restriction is when a leader caretaker has committed a violent action without it being in self-defense. In that case, the particular leader caretaker is restricted from access. Checks and balances will ensure offending leader caretakers are de-selected and replacements made.

Choose Your Primes

An elitist belief system keeps all others in chains. Adherence to injustice promotes terrorism. The ones in power hide behind this belief system. Choose a different belief system. Choose adherence to sentient and wise leader caretakers. Choose your primes wisely. They are unique and so are we.

Nature's Sanctuary Domains

There will be defined vast sanctuary domains for life generating organisms to thrive on Earth so that no species are extinguished due to sentient catastrophic behaviors. These domains will also be used as a benchmark for sentient interactions on non-sanctuary domains. Sentients will not extinguish life so that they will be allowed to inhabit all of Earth. The only interactions by sentients are very limited non-intrusive visitations that are monitored by sanctuary caretakers who are given the auspices caretaker keys to the sanctuaries. Choose them wisely.

Atonement Activities

By participating in prime directive creation activities, it will aid one in one's atonement since one will participate in wise and more effective issue resolutions. Is this important to you?

Entity Awareness Path

By establishing and promoting primes, an entity will evolve towards a higher level of awareness. This evolution may not be apparent in this moment in time. However, time will prove the evolution to be dramatic and profound!

Thoughts and Affirmations

Know your Primes

Work with your primes. Have your opinions known to them.

Condemn Not!

You don't actually condemn me. It is reflective. You condemn yourself.

The End to Condemnations

A nation-state that condemns will be extinguished. It will condemn no more!

The Life of Primes

A prime has a life of its own. You can be a part of this life.

No One is Alone

When we come together as primes, no one is left alone.

Being Sentient

No law will exist that negates an entity for being sentient.

"What-Ifs"

Speculations on "what-ifs" regarding the shaping of historical belief systems are not promoted during transition to pentarchy primes. Pentarchy prime disclosure of prime directives to its members is the source of our strength.

Metamorphose into something greater!

With primes, one will find one's self.

It is a Matter of Time

A system that condemns cannot long endure.

It Starts With One

I am one entity. I need four more to make a prime. This is the start to the propagation of primes.

Start by Building Primes

We don't need institutions. We need caretakers. When primes reach a pentacle, it is of prime celebration!

Tipping the Scale

Your one vote, one action, could make the difference in tipping the scale in pentarchy prime installment.

Prime Rules!

Leader caretakers are supreme to all other systems.

Prime Foundation and Beyond

The Fallacies of Triage

By adopting the framework of pentarchy prime, your activities will expose the fallacies of the historical triage belief systems, which have the premise of advancing feudal lord rules and the distinction of the elite with their exclusive privileges over the masses.

Break the Cycle of Land Wars

One may consider the notion that the need for transformation can be put off indefinitely. To hold onto the framework of land lords will promote land wars indefinitely. Understand the true nature of entities to be set free is the same as fighting for land, even though it was not apparent at the time. With the framework of pentarchy primes, no land boundaries are defined. Hence, no need to fight for land and hence, for freedom. To fight for land is more than the exclusion of entities. History has shown that in every single case, slavery, terrorism, and genocide are the resultant events. Choose to give governance power to the many and not to the few elite.

Micro-View Governments

History is clear. Governments can only deal with other governments. Translation, the elite can only deal with other elite groups. Another way of looking at this is that "micro-view" governments can only interact with other "micro-view" governments. Responsibility for decisions is the actions that are the result of these decisions, which can be defused and hidden throughout governmental institutions. With pentarchy primes, there is no diffusion. The selection of leader caretakers is made by all. Choose your leader caretakers wisely.

Prime Construction

Do not be concern about convincing entities that are not interested in the framework of pentarchy primes. They will not be aware that a healing wave of prime construction is taking place in full view. The triumph is when prime directives will require them to comply or be removed from their positions and privileges withheld. Complying will be swift.

By nourishing and promoting primes, we will have the most effective conflict-resolution-solving framework ever achieved.

There is a Choice

Pentarchy Primes are only for those who wish to elevate themselves from slavery and servitude that have been enforced by feudal lords. What choice will you make?

Sentient Responsible Organization

We are a sentient responsible organization, not a political action one. This distinction will be readily refreshing in time.

Controlling Interest

Do not be discouraged that the framework of pentarchy primes will take years to bring to collective consciousness. Take comfort with the knowledge that with anything, when folks are free to choose a higher evolved prime framework, then it takes just fifty-one percent of the vote in a historical voting establishments to gain a more unobstructed controlling interest. This will provide us with the critical awareness to take universal hold. This sentient framework will be implemented everywhere from that moment on. This will truly be the Nexus Moment.

Nexus Prime at any Degree

Nexus prime can occur at any degree. With premiere founders, we will use the pent-degree pentarchy prime to be the Nexus Birth of Universal Directives. Each degree ascension prime thereafter will be to re-affirm or refine these directives. Failure by any member of society to comply will be noted and prime decisions recorded. It may appear that an entity is getting away with non-compliance. However in time, all debts will be cleared with compliance.

Nexus Fundamental Changes

Fundamental nexus tenets and principles can only be modified by the unanimous decision of the nexus prime leader caretakers and the plurality opinions of the degree minus-five of foundation primes within the nexus prime. With the event of having the unanimous opinion of the nexus prime leader caretakers, a significant tenet change request is made known to all. With the participation of the degree minus-five of foundation prime members within the nexus prime, the checks and balances are preserved.

Truth Discoveries

The truth is what will always be pursued and expounded. It will not be done in a manner of convenience and cost effectiveness when very harmful acts are being investigated. Determining the true causes for the acts will bring to the fore opportunities to remove harmful generating environments. This refinement will truly promote peace and tranquillity.

Sentient Life-Forms Recognized

Human form will be one of many sentient life forms or species in a greater society. It did take society a very long time to acknowledge that other races of man are part of a greater society. To advance to the next level of an even greater society is to apply the same characteristics and attributes applied to human form evaluations so as to admit other candidate species with the same degree of protection from execution or annihilation. The spawning for this greater society is to eliminate ALL references to members of society being subjects or property of a feudal state. Decisions are made by wise caretakers and not by institutions as they are currently defined, which exist in form and not substance. Institutions are to be instruments and extensions of caretakers. They are to carry out the opinions of our wisest caretakers.

Prime Foundation Specifications

This book provides specifications for any prime to operate in, even when developing primes are not aware of each other. Should two or more developing primes make contact, this book handles the ascension prime as well. This is a great feature of primes because the nexus is the limit.

Closing Remarks

Once there were Guerrilla "Freedom Fighters"

Historically, the once most powerful nation on earth was a guerrilla terrorist regime fighting the Great Feudal Empires of its time. Later in history, the "Geneva Convention" dictated the terms regarding prisoners of war (POW) during wartime. This is the result of a collective nation-states decree. The decree applies primarily to opposing nation-state solders. Conclusion, non-solders that take up arms are considered guerrillas and are not protected. This is hypocrisy since all countries were founded by guerrilla activities. Therefore, guerrillas cannot be considered terrorists or the same claim must be universally applied regarding "established" nation-states. Choose to terrorize no more.

When the military is used for defensive or offensive purposes, then those entities that are captured because of their participation in the conflict are to be considered as prisoners of war (POW). Only when civilian police forces are involved is the term POW not used. However, this definition will be a moot point once nation-states expire. The solution is to dismantle all land-based nation-states. The need for guerrilla or terrorist activity, depending on your point-of-view, will no longer be needed. Later in history, there will be no land claims to fight over. Land will be auspices of all sentients.

Living and Breathing Foundation Prime

Over time, this book will be a living and breathing one due to revisions that will be incorporated as a more complete set of nexus tenets and foundation principles is defined or established ones refined based on discovery and learning activities.

Timely Responses

Historical trilateral systems; legislative, executive, and judicial; waits for tragedies to occur first before acting on them. Wise decisions are not done by this reactionary mechanism (machine). Using their historical ways of adversarial processes, uncovering truths were drowned out. There is, in general, no rapid response team on the scene of grave harmful events. In a pentarchy prime framework, the nexus prime has ultimate responsibility to ensure that effective truth discovery activities do take place and the outcomes published.

Law is Reflective

For those who do not think that the laws maim, torture, oppress, etc., guess again. Do your own research and discover for yourself that the methods that are being used to accomplish them have been kept hidden from the non-elite. The law is criminal when it condemns. The law is reflective. See for yourself.

Exclusion Implosion

Historically, power was derived through exclusion and through the labors of others. That kind of forced attainment will expire, if not already. The propagation of primes will ensure that exclusions do not exist.

Terrorism no more!

This original author is working to eliminate government-sanctioned terrorism in all its form. Forms of terrorism will be exposed no matter how deeply hidden they may appear to be. In time, there will be terrorism no more. Will you be there with the rest of us?

Primes Engulf the Landscape

Create Primes, then watch as primes engulf the unsuspecting "old guards" and "landscapes" as more and more of the "nation-states" get absorbed. One by one, the treaty organizations will expire and be replaced with prime directives. The need to maintain military hardware and personnel will dwindle and then be disbanded because there will be no more "land boundaries" to protect.

Society of Self-determination

Pentarchy prime framework is not a political party. It is a vast societal pool of sentient entities resuming their right of self-determination.

Impending Implosion

A society based on condemnation will implode. It will not long endure.

Rogue Nation-States

The belief in nation-states permits rogue states to hold the majority at bay. Primes encompass and embrace the entire umbrella pool so that no entity is overlooked.

It is "Within Reason"

It is not unreasonable to expect decision-making bodies to make decisions that would benefit all of society. If any confess that little can be done to make this so, then they are not that great after all. Maintenance and propping up of feudal systems are their primary objectives. We can choose to promote the preferred path. This guidebook will assist.

It Starts With One

This book describes the establishment of foundation primes. This birth begins with the sentient awareness of entities. Will you be one of them?

Nation-State Fall Back

The framework of land-based nation-states cannot long endure and evolve into a higher framework. The "evolution" can only lead to the return to more barbarous feudal states whereby ethnic cleansing is the law for instant wealth and "new land" ownership.

Prevention of Total Annihilation

Retaining the framework of nation-state as ever-greater technological advances are made will lead to total annihilation by these "technological advances". How great can it be when its use returns all to rubble?

Individual Recognition

By promoting individualism by the nation-state makes it possible to extinguish an entity. With pentarchy primes, a pool will have to be extinguished. This is a very great feat unless mass destruction is promoted. If the nation-state does in fact do it, the result is its implosion. Hence, there is safety in numbers.

What took so long?

Time will pass and entities born in the not so distant future will look at this contemporary period of time, as of the writing of this guidebook version of primes, and ask what took society so long to adopt the Charter of Primes? They will view the detractors and force resisters not in a favorable light. In fact, they may even be scorned for their actions and in-actions.

Out in the Cold

Pentarchy primes will not initially be well received. However over time, the repeated demonstrations of decision making by all entities will be realized and be well received in greater numbers. The naysayers will discover that they are "out in the cold" by their own activities.

See the Future Today

When all is said and done regarding the planting and nurturing of primes, future sojourners will find it difficult to understand why society took so long to embrace a universal member growth-developing framework as pentarchy primes. Can you see the future today? It is all around us.

Premier Founders

The first five to the fifth power members will be given the designation of "Premier Founders". This is a great honor because their resolve and stamina have changed the course of societal existence forever! Development towards a higher level of awareness is assured.

Guidebook Ready!

This book is written to be available when the time comes to evolve, as a society, to something greater. It may appear that much time has past and nothing is happening requiring this guidebook. However, the time will be ripe for the seeds described in this book to germinate. It will then catch on like wildfire as artifact feudal systems implode. A system based on shifting landmasses is shaky indeed and may ultimately return to the sea.

Book Fund

A fund will be established to help pay for copies of this book in those cases when the interested person meets a hardship need level, which is defined as subsistence or below.

Disclaimer

For those who need a disclaimer in order to continue to exist in their framework, any usage of pentarchy prime framework specified in manual scripts and books are based on the interpretation of the readers and users of them. This fact must be publicly stated for the reader and user. The author does not attest to any accurate interpretation made

F. Dot

by any reader or user. Her actions are self-
determined.

Spectacular Results

Allow primes to flourish. You will be pleasantly
surprised with its spectacular results.

Primes Endure!

Primes endure!

Bulletins

Revisions

Within a short period of time after the initial publishing of this book, the changes (refinements) will be found to be minimal. Over a longer period of time and after much discoveries and experiences, the refinements may be somewhat more significant. However, do not be surprised if the pentarchy prime framework and related tenets and principles remain largely intact.

Living Foundation Guide

Minor revisions for this book are scheduled in five years of published date. Input from prime members is welcomed and appreciated.

Comprehensive embellishments pertaining to this book is scheduled in twenty-five years of the original published date. I recommend that umbrella primes pend-degree and greater reach be the primary authors for the twenty-fifth year revision, which will most likely be expansions on the basic premise.

Your Feedback and Suggestions Welcomed Here

I welcome your feedback and suggestions from any prime member. Your suggestions will be reviewed and may be incorporated in an updated version of this book five years from the original published date.

When feedback indicates certain passages of this book requires a greater degree of clarity, the addition of tenets, or the addition of prime guiding principles then a bulletin will be forthcoming so that there are not delays in disseminating this information. Should there be many bulletins then an updated book will be published. It will be another twenty-five years whereby much will have been learned and articulated, at which time the author relinquishes authorship to the nexus prime umbrella.

About the Author

Like other spiritual entities, the author has gone through life seeking a greater understanding regarding everything that surrounds her. Often times, much searching, studying, and thinking took place towards this greater understanding. It was not sufficient that she lead a comfortable life, but one that moves her closer to All-That-Is (ATI). Major life events tested her resolve in choosing not to be like sheep in going through the motions of a "normal" life. This notion was unacceptable. She chose instead to challenge the accepted dogma of the day and accept nothing less then a sentient awareness-promoting environment. With this understanding came responsibilities. Her calling became clear. It compelled her to pass on these insights to all that are receptive to this greater understanding. Her book is the culmination of decades of active pursuits in universal insights and how those wonderful insights can have practical application in promoting a sentient world.

Written Now

This book is being written now so that when major Earth changes occur,
this handbook will allow order to quickly be established. Relying on
arcane institutions will extend harsh pain and suffering. This is
unnecessary. We have the capability to provide caring and humane
treatment towards each other. Do not be fooled when others make the
claim that the current belief systems are the only ones. Dare to choose a
more all encompassing one.

Blue Print for Development

This book is provided as a blue print for an optimum environment for
advancing entity pools' development. One of the purposes is to describe
a framework for all sentients to be included, if the will be there. The
framework is one of inclusion and not to be limited to a small percent of
the society pool. Are you up to it?

Need a Disclaimer?

We can customize a disclaimer for you if you like should you find the
words that are used in this book disturbing. The journey is truly yours to
take should you choose to take a chance on something that will be quite
magnificent! Do you need a disclaimer or will you dare to choose?

ISBN 1-4107-7438-4

9 781410 774385